Nigeria

Nigeria

BY LURA ROGERS SEAVEY

Enchantment of the World™
Second Series

CHILDREN'S PRESS®

An Imprint of Scholastic Inc.

Frontispiece: **Coming of age ceremony for an Ondo girl**

Consultant: Omolade Adunbi, Assistant Professor, Department of Afroamerican and African Studies, University of Michigan, Ann Arbor

Please note: All statistics are as up-to-date as possible at the time of publication.

Book production by The Design Lab

Library of Congress Cataloging-in-Publication Data
Names: Rogers Seavey, Lura, author.
Title: Nigeria / by Lura Rogers Seavey.
Description: New York, NY : Children's Press, an imprint of Scholastic Inc., [2016] | Series: Enchantment of the world | Includes bibliographical references and index.
Identifiers: LCCN 2016000349 | ISBN 9780531218860 (library binding)
Subjects: LCSH: Nigeria—Juvenile literature.
Classification: LCC DT515.22 .R65 2016 | DDC 966.9—dc23
LC record available at http://lccn.loc.gov/2016000349

1 2 3 4 5 6 7 8 9 10 R 26 25 24 23 22 21 20 19 18 17

A drill at Afi Mountain Wildlife Sanctuary

Contents

Left to right: **Niger River, baobab tree, white-throated monkey, market, rural house**

CHAPTER 1

A World of Potential

NIGERIA IS A LAND OF INCREDIBLE DIVERSITY. Located on the Gulf of Guinea in West Africa, it is home to volcanic mountains, dry plains, lush rain forests, and the rich Niger River delta. With the largest population of any African country, Nigeria is home to a wide variety of people from different ethnic and religious backgrounds.

These many different groups have achieved much throughout history. More than two thousand years ago, people of the Nok culture created lifelike heads out of clay. Later, the Igbo, Yoruba, and Benin peoples created sophisticated metal sculptures. Hundreds of years ago, the Hausa people built walled cities on important trade routes. Today, Nigeria has the largest economy in Africa.

As a nation, Nigeria has faced many challenges. Its diverse people are bound by political borders, yet they are separated

Opposite: **Schoolchildren in Jos, in central Nigeria. More than 40 percent of Nigerians are less than fifteen years old.**

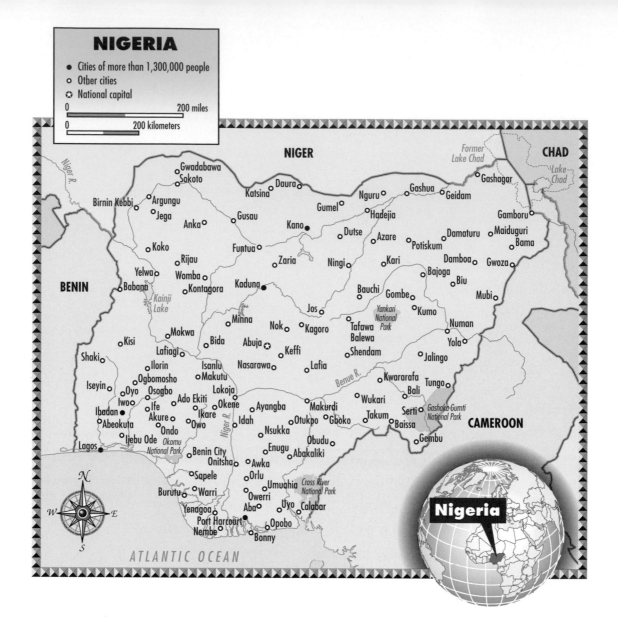

NIGERIA

- ● Cities of more than 1,300,000 people
- ○ Other cities
- ⊕ National capital

0 _____ 200 miles

0 _____ 200 kilometers

NIGER

CHAD

Former Lake Chad

Lake Chad

Niger R.

Gwadabawa
Sokoto
Daura
Gashagar
Birnin Kebbi
Argungu
Katsina
Nguru
Gashua
Geidam
Jega
Gumel
Gamboru
Anka
Gusau
Kano
Hadejia
Maiduguri
Koko
Dutse
Azare
Potiskum
Damaturu
Bama
Rijau
Zaria
Ningi
Kari
Damboa
Gwoza
Yelwa
Womba
Ningi
Bajoga
Biu
BENIN
Babana
Kontagora
Kaduna
Bauchi
Gombe
Mubi
Kainji Lake
Minna
Nok
Kagoro
Tafawa Balewa
Kumo
Numan
Mokwa
Jos
Yankari National Park
Yola
Kisi
Bida
Abuja
Keffi
Shendam
Jalingo
Lafiagi
Nasarawa
Lafia
Shaki
Ilorin
Isanlu
Makutu
Kwararafa
Tungo
Iseyin
Ogbomosho
Lokoja
Benue R.
Bali
Oyo
Osogbo
Ado Ekiti
Okene
Ayangba
Makurdi
Wukari
Serti
Gashaka-Gumti National Park
Iwoo
Ife
Ikare
Idah
Otukpo
Gboko
Takum
Baissa
CAMEROON
Ibadan
Akure
Owo
Nsukka
Obudu
Gembu
Abeokuta
Ondo
Ijebu Ode
Okomu National Park
Enugu
Abakaliki
Lagos
Benin City
Onitsha
Awka
Cross River National Park
Sapele
Orlu
Umuahia
Burutu
Warri
Owerri
Yenagoa
Aba
Uyo
Calabar
Port Harcourt
Opobo
Nembe
Bonny

ATLANTIC OCEAN

N W E S

Nigeria

by geography, culture, and strong beliefs. The varied groups have often been in conflict with one another.

As in many parts of the world, war and conflict occurred inside Nigeria long before outsiders came along. But for the people of West Africa, the arrival of foreigners brought one of the most devastating periods imaginable. Between the 1500s and the 1800s, the Atlantic slave trade ripped millions of people from their homes and families.

Strife has continued through the centuries. Today, the young Republic of Nigeria faces sometimes violent conflict among its people. The land holds vast resources, particularly oil, but the country struggles to find a way to keep all the wealth from those resources from falling into the hands of a small number of people. The country has a population of young, determined people who want to see a better world for their children and help their nation rise from its difficult past and heal its current wounds.

A police officer directs traffic at a market in Lagos, the largest city in Nigeria. Lagos is a bustling place, the fastest growing city in Africa.

CHAPTER 2

Top to Bottom

FROM DESERTS AND PLAINS TO THE WATERLOGGED Niger Delta and steamy rain forests, Nigeria is a varied land. As a large nation, it has a wide range of land features with varying weather across many regions. These factors affect the people who live there and also how they use the land.

Nigeria is located in West Africa, with its southern border on the Gulf of Guinea, in the Atlantic Ocean. To the west, it borders Benin Republic, and to the north the Republic of Niger. It shares its eastern border with Cameroon, and the northeast corner borders Chad. Nigeria covers an area of 356,669 square miles (923,768 square kilometers), which is roughly twice the size of California.

Opposite: **Gurara Falls in the central part of Nigeria is one of the country's major tourist attractions.**

Nigeria's Geographic Features

Area: 356,669 square miles (923,768 sq km)

Highest Elevation: Chappal Waddi, at 7,936 feet (2,419 m) above sea level

Lowest Elevation: Sea level along the coast

Longest River: Niger River, 730 miles (1,175 km) within Nigeria

Largest Reservoir: Kainji Lake, 480 square miles (1,243 sq km)

Largest Lake: Lake Chad, 521 square miles (1,350 sq km)

Average High Temperature: In Lagos, 90°F (32°C) in January; 82°F (28°C) in July

Average Low Temperature: In Lagos, 72°F (22°C) in January; 72°F (22°C) in July

Average Annual Precipitation: Varies, from 20 inches (50 cm) in the far north to 120 inches (300 cm) in the southeast

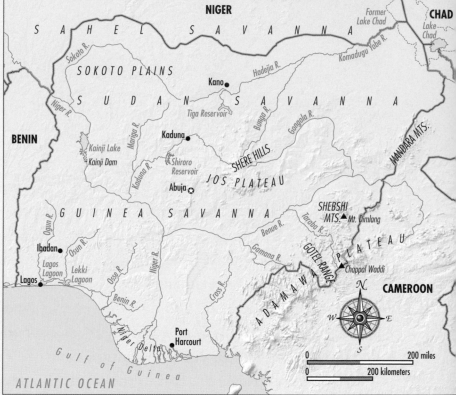

Nigeria's Waterways

Nigeria gets its name from the Niger River, the third-longest river in Africa, running a total of 2,600 miles (4,200 kilometers). It enters Nigeria in the northwest, and then runs south across the country to sea. It is fed by many tributaries, or smaller rivers. The largest is the Benue, which enters Nigeria from the east. Because the Benue does not have any waterfalls or rapids, it can be used for water transport from the border to the center of the country.

The Niger, however, is broken up by rapids and waterfalls, which keep it from being a major water route. Instead, the force of its flow is used in many places to generate hydroelectric power. This requires building dams that create artificial lakes, or reservoirs.

Kainji Lake was created on the upper Niger when the Kainji Dam was built. Today, the lake covers up to about 500

In some parts of southern Niger, boating is the easiest way to travel.

Kainji Dam

The Kainji Dam is the largest dam on the Niger River, at 1,800 feet (550 m) wide and 215 feet (66 m) high. It was built between 1964 and 1968, creating the Kainji Lake reservoir. The construction of the dam forced about fifty thousand people to move because their land was going to be flooded by the lake. The government built housing in other areas for many of those who had been displaced. Kainji Dam generates hydroelectric power, doubles as a bridge, and helps control water levels downstream.

square miles (1,300 square kilometers) and reaches 39 feet (12 meters) deep when the river is at its highest. The lake provides water for local irrigation, and is a major fishing area.

The Niger eventually spreads out into the Niger Delta, which is Africa's largest delta and the third largest in the world, covering 14,000 square miles (36,000 sq km), an area larger than the U.S. state of Maryland. In this large basin, the river branches off into many smaller ones that then empty into the Gulf of Guinea. The mouth of the delta consumes around 200 miles (320 km) of the coastline. The Niger Delta is the source of Nigeria's wealth. In 1956, oil was discovered in the delta. Today, Nigeria is the largest oil-producing nation in Africa.

Lake Chad sits in the northeastern corner of Nigeria, forming part of the border with Cameroon and Chad. It was once one of the largest lakes in Africa, but over the past fifty years it has shrunk by more than 90 percent. Many factors have contributed to the lake's decreasing size, including irrigation.

Nigeria and the other surrounding countries have been using the lake and the rivers that feed it to irrigate cropland, and more water is being used than can be replaced. Some studies also suggest climate change is responsible for the lake shrinking. Lake Chad is currently estimated to have a surface area of 521 square miles (1,350 sq km).

Higher Ground

Nigeria has three mountain ranges. They lie in the northeastern part of the country, forming a large part of the border. The Mandara Mountains, the northernmost range, are located

A view of the Niger Delta from space. The delta, crisscrossed by many rivers, makes up about 7.5 percent of the area of the country.

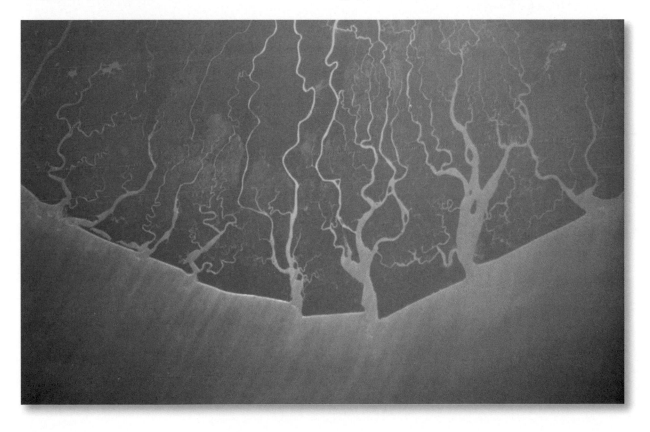

Clouds hang over a mountainous region in southwestern Nigeria.

primarily in the neighboring country of Cameroon. About halfway down the eastern border, the Shebshi Mountains begin, jutting into the savanna at a northwest angle for around 100 miles (160 km). This range includes Mount Dimlang, which rises to 6,699 feet (2,042 m) above sea level, making it the second-highest point in Nigeria.

To the south of this range, bordering Cameroon, is the Gotel range. It is surrounded by a high plateau and is home to the country's tallest peak, Chappal Waddi, which reaches 7,936 feet (2,419 m) above sea level. In the local language, Chappal Waddi means "Death Mountain." The high elevations make the climate cooler than other parts of the country. In July, for example, the mountain peak reaches an average temperature of 69 degrees Fahrenheit (21 degrees Celsius) during the day, while Lagos reaches an average of 82°F (28°C).

Plateau lands occupy much of the northern half of the country and there is a smaller plateau region in the southwest. A plateau, sometimes called a tableland, is an area of mostly flat land that stands well above its surroundings. These are often separated abruptly from the lower elevations by sharp cliff-like drop-offs called escarpments.

Nigeria's largest plateau is the Jos Plateau, which lies in the center of the country. The Jos Plateau has an average elevation of 4,200 feet (1,280 m) above sea level, but in the Shere Hills, which lie on the plateau, the land reaches heights of 6,000 feet (1,800 m). A large portion of the plateau's surface is made of ancient lava from the region's many extinct volcanoes.

For a long time, the Jos Plateau was Africa's most important tin-mining center. It used to be widely forested, but most of the trees have been cleared and the land is now mostly grassy. Although overused by farmers, this land does produce staple crops. The weather is temperate because of the altitude, averaging between 70 and 77°F (21 and 25°C).

Nigeria's Largest Cities

Lagos (below) is Nigeria's largest city, with a population of more than 13 million. It was the capital city before the government headquarters were moved to Abuja in 1991. Lagos is known locally as Eko. The Portuguese named it Lagos when they started trading with the local population in the 1400s. The city, which is made up of many islands, began as a Portuguese trade port. Today, it remains Nigeria's major port. It is also Nigeria's cultural center, the site of the Nigerian National Museum, the National Library, and the University of Lagos. The city's dominant ethnic group is the Yoruba people.

Kano is the second-largest city in Nigeria, with a population of about 3.5 million. It is one of the main urban centers in the northern part of the country. Kano has a long history as a center of trade. The Old City is surrounded by walls that date to the fifteenth century. Its major sites include the Emir's Palace (above), the Great Mosque, and the Kurmi Market. The dominant ethnic groups in Kano are the Hausas and Fulanis.

Nigeria's third-largest city, Ibadan, is home to more than 3 million people. It lies about 100 miles (160 km) north of Lagos. A major center for trade, Ibadan is known for its many markets that sell both imports from the coast and a variety of local crafts like pottery and *adire*, or tie-dyed fabric. The city's dominant ethnic group is the Yorubas.

Men ride through a
sandstorm in Nigeria.
Strong winds blow across
the dry northern part
of the country between
November and March.

Lying Low

The far north and far south have low-lying plains. Less rain
falls in the north than in other parts of the country, and the
dry season is much longer. In many places, rivers slow to a
trickle or dry up completely. The hottest part of the country is
the northern plains. This region experiences a hot, dust-filled
wind called the harmattan. In the plains, summer temperatures reach an average of 104°F (40°C), with some areas
getting as hot as 111°F (44°C).

The southern plains are much more humid, gathering
moisture from the ocean. The coastline stretches 530 miles
(853 km) along the Gulf of Guinea. Temperatures in this
region are steady year-round, with an average low of 79°F
(26°C) and average high of 82°F (28°C). The low plains of
the south become saturated with water in the rainy season,
which brings between 80 and 120 inches (200 and 300 centi-
meters) of rain each year.

CHAPTER 3

The Wild World

THE CLIMATES OF NORTHERN AND SOUTHERN NIGERIA are quite different from each other, so the landscapes and growth in each region are also different. In addition, different plants thrive in the coastal areas than in inland regions. Most of Nigeria is covered by forests or savannas, grasslands with only occasional trees.

Opposite: **Much of the Jos Plateau is farmland. Common crops include grains, potatoes, and yams.**

Vast Savannas

Spreading across Nigeria's middle is its largest grassland area, Guinea Savanna, which covers nearly half the country. The southern part of the savanna boasts taller grass and more trees, because the region receives the most rain. Parts of the savanna have been damaged by human activity. For example, in some places, the trees and other plants have been cleared to make more land for agriculture.

Farther north is the Sudan Savanna, which covers about one-fourth of the country, reaching from the western Sokoto

Baobab trees have extremely thick trunks. The trees store water in their trunks, which allows them to survive long dry periods.

Plains through the northern central highlands. It has a lower annual rainfall than the Guinea Savanna, and its dry season lasts six to nine months. As a result, this savanna has shorter grass and fewer trees, which are often stunted by drought. Because this region has some of northern Nigeria's densest population, much of the land has been stripped for planting crops and raising cattle. The most common types of trees in this region are the acacia, the baobab, and the silk cotton tree.

In the far north, and at the edge of the great Sahara desert and close to Lake Chad, is the Sahel Savanna, the driest of Nigeria's savannas. Grasses here are shorter, only about 3 feet (1 m) high, and patches of grass are often separated by bare sand dunes. The most common trees in this area are acacia and date palms. Farming is only possible where land can be irrigated from Lake Chad, which is slowly drying up.

Tropical Forests

Mixed with Nigeria's savannas are forests, which change in character from the inland areas to the coast, becoming the most lush in the humid south. Near the coast are saltwater swamps, where mangrove trees grow thickly in areas where salty seawater mixes with the freshwater from rivers and creeks. Mangroves grow with their tangled roots partly in and partly out of the water. Coconut palms often grow in a fringe behind these mangrove swamps. Farther inland is a belt of freshwater swamp forest, which thrives in the wet climate and plentiful fresh water from rivers before they mix with the tidal seawater.

The trees that grow in freshwater swamps along the lagoons and creeks in the Niger Delta are hard to reach, so not many have been cut down. Raffia palms are the most common trees in this area, while oil palms and large Iroko trees grow in the better-drained places.

In the rain forest, tropical evergreen trees grow surrounded by a thick undergrowth of shrubs and a tangle of climbing vines. Hundreds of plant species thrive in these damp forests. The vines and underbrush protect the big trees, which often

Thousands of different
plant species live in the
Nigerian rain forest.

grow as tall as 200 feet (60 m). This belt of luxuriant rain forest stretches from the western border with Benin Republic, along the Niger and Benue Rivers into southeastern Nigeria. Although these forests produce valuable woods like mahogany and walnut, they are mostly safe from cutting because they are hard to get to. These rain forests are not entirely safe from destruction by humans, though. Large areas of the lower growth have been cleared to make room for farming, especially in the east where some forests have been replaced by oil palm plantations and vegetable farms.

In addition to savannas and forests, Nigeria has some plateau areas in the central and eastern regions where mountain plants grow.

Protecting the Forests

A century ago, two-thirds of Nigeria was covered in forest. By the 1990s, forests had diminished to covering less than 20 percent of the land. Today, forest covers only about 10 percent of Nigeria. Some of the forest has been cleared for farming, but much of the wood has been cut for use in cooking fires. When the mangrove trees that grow along the coast are cut, the coastal areas are put in serious danger of flooding.

Some forest areas, especially in the southwest, have been protected by national parks and conservation rules. But much of Nigeria's population is poor, and wood is the cheapest source of fuel. This makes it difficult for the nation to prioritize conservation over the immediate needs of the people.

A woman in the Niger Delta region transports firewood on her bicycle. Roughly two-thirds of Nigerians rely on wood to fuel their cooking fires.

National Parks and Reserves

Each of Nigeria's national parks protects endangered plants and animals, and preserves the wild environment they live in. Here are some of the most important:

Cross River National Park, in the south, is Nigeria's last great rain forest reserve. Thirty percent of its land is forested. This park provides the habitat for the Cross River gorilla and the rare drill monkey.

Gashaka-Gumti National Park (below), in northeastern Nigeria, is the largest and most scenic of Nigeria's national parks. Among the mountains in the park is

Nigeria's highest point, Chappal Waddi. The mountain forests are habitat for chimpanzees, giant elands, and many other creatures.

Okomu National Park, near Benin City, is Nigeria's smallest national park, but it has a lot of wildlife. The white-throated monkey (above), one of the world's rarest monkey species, lives here alongside forest elephants, buffalo, and leopards.

Yankari National Park, in northeastern Nigeria, is well known for its wildlife, especially for its African bush elephant herd of about 350, the largest in West Africa. Baboons, hyenas, bushbuck, buffalo, waterbuck, lions, and leopards all share this reserve, which also has a large variety of birds.

Animal Life

A great variety of animals once lived in Nigeria's forests and savannas. Today, however, most large animals, such as elephants, giraffes, and lions, are limited to national parks and other protected places. Crocodiles and hippopotamuses still live in the rivers. And smaller creatures such as porcupines can be found in the forests. Large birds such as vultures and kites soar through the air, while guinea fowl rustle through the grasses of the savanna.

Crocodiles hunt by ambush. They sometimes almost completely submerge themselves in the water, sitting quietly so prey will come near.

The hartebeest is one of the more than twenty species of antelope that live in Nigeria. Both male and female hartebeests have horns.

The animal life is diminished in part because of the destruction of their forest and savanna habitat. In addition, wild animals and birds are hunted as a source of meat for people who have few sources of food. This is an especially serious problem for species found only in Nigeria, such as Sclater's guenon, the white-throated monkey, and the red colobus monkey, all of which are facing possible extinction. Antelopes are hunted extensively for meat, endangering the future of several species.

Other endangered animals in Nigeria include the African spurred tortoise, one of the world's largest tortoises. It was once common in the northern Sahel region and is now rarely found in the wild. Several of Nigeria's 940 recorded species of bird are endangered, including the African gray parrot.

Nigeria's Most Endangered Animals

More than two dozen types of mammals in Nigeria are endangered or vulnerable to extinction. These include:

West African lion: Fifty years ago about two hundred thousand lions roamed Africa. Today, 90 percent of those have disappeared, and only about thirty-four are left in all of Nigeria.

Cross River gorilla: These gorillas (below) were once common in Nigeria's forests, but now only about three hundred remain in Nigeria and Cameroon combined.

White-throated guenon: Also called the red-bellied monkey, these creatures are found in the rain forests of Nigeria and Benin. They have been so heavily hunted for their unusual red and white fur that there now remains only a small colony near the Niger River.

Red-eared guenon: A monkey found in tropical forests of Nigeria and neighboring Cameroon and Equatorial Guinea, this guenon is near extinction because many have been captured and sold illegally as pets.

CHAPTER 4

Nigeria's Rocky Path

HUMANS ORIGINATED ON THE CONTINENT OF Africa. Fossils of early humans dating back as far as 9000 BCE have been found in the region that is now Nigeria. Early humans were nomadic hunters and gatherers who left behind little evidence of their way of life. As peoples settled, their cultures reflected the resources and environment of the land they called home. Many states and regions of modern Nigeria are named for these different groups, and some of the traditional cultures still exist.

Opposite: **People of the Nok culture made beautiful sculptures of clay. Experts believe that the figures were shaped by hand and the clay was then carved away, in the same way a person carves wood.**

Many Cultures

The Nok people settled on the Jos Plateau as early as 500 BCE. They occupied this region for seven hundred years. They knew how to cultivate crops and raised cattle. The Nok people were

Kano, in what is now northern Nigeria, was one of the Hausa states. It became a major center of trade.

named after the village where their pottery was first discovered. They are best known for their terra-cotta (clay) sculptures, especially those of lifelike heads. Alongside these sculptures, archaeologists found early ironworking tools and many brass items, including jewelry and ornamental pieces.

In the plains to the north, the Hausa states were well-organized settlements. Each had its own walled city and a political system ruled by kings. This region had many markets because it was centrally located on several trade routes, including north-

One of the most powerful leaders among the Hausas was Queen Amina. She became the ruler of Zaria, one of the Hausa states, in the 1500s. Amina was a legendary fighter and military strategist who led her people to conquer many other territories. She controlled trade routes and helped develop her kingdom.

ern routes to the Sahara and local routes to the forested areas. Because of their valuable location, the Hausa states often had to defend themselves from invasions by neighboring states.

One of the invaders was the Borno people. They had left their territory north of Lake Chad after repeated attacks from another group. They went in search of a new place to settle and ended up west of the lake. They eventually became part of the nearby Kanem kingdom. This kingdom included women in the political system, which was unusual for the time.

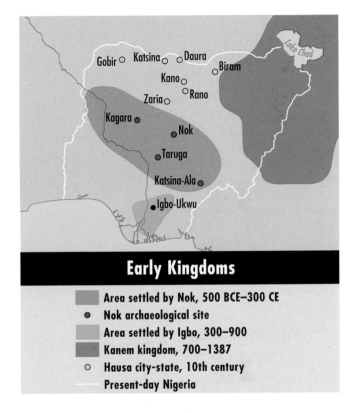

Early Kingdoms

- Area settled by Nok, 500 BCE–300 CE
- ● Nok archaeological site
- Area settled by Igbo, 300–900
- Kanem kingdom, 700–1387
- ○ Hausa city-state, 10th century
- — Present-day Nigeria

Around 900 CE the Igbo-Ukwu, later known simply as the Igbos, were settling in the southeast. Unlike the people of northern settlements, the Igbos did not have a centralized government system, despite having a large population. The Igbos were led by the *eze nri*, a spiritual leader like a priest. He was held in esteem like a king but had no actual governing power. Governmental duties were handled at the village level.

Yorubaland

The Yoruba people settled in the southwest, an area known as Yorubaland. This was an attractive region because of its fertile soil, nearby forests, and convenient access to the sea. The Yorubas were divided into many different groups, which became kingdoms. The Yoruba states included the Ile-Ife and Oyo peoples.

The Ile-Ife people lived in forested regions south of the Oyo, in present-day Osun State. The region where the Ile-Ife lived is considered the cradle of Yoruba civilization. All people of Yoruba descent trace their origin here. This region,

The Igbo people were accomplished metalworkers. This ram's head dates to the ninth century CE.

This metal sculpture of an Oni was created by the Ile-Ife people about eight hundred years ago. Ile-Ife sculpture is renowned for its elegant naturalism.

and the city of Ife in particular, was considered a holy place where many gods lived, and the Ile-Ife king, called the Oni, was believed to be a god. For centuries, the Yoruba states have used lineage from these kings to determine who is entitled to be king. Ile-Ife artifacts dating from 900 CE to 1400 CE remain, including life-size terra-cotta sculptures, bronze work, and stone sculptures.

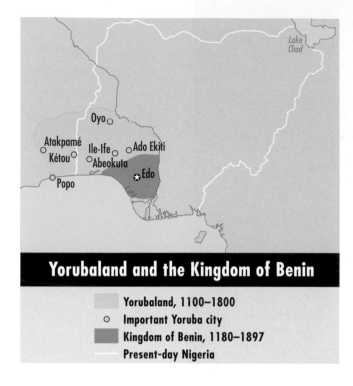

Yorubaland and the Kingdom of Benin

- Yorubaland, 1100–1800
- ○ Important Yoruba city
- Kingdom of Benin, 1180–1897
- Present-day Nigeria

The Oyo established their territory in the 1300s, in the savanna west of the Niger River and north of the forest. They were well positioned at a meeting point for traders from the north and south, and they soon became a powerful empire, with territory that extended into parts of what is today's Benin Republic, Togo, and Ghana. The Oyo traded with the northerners for horses. By 1600, they had established a large and well-trained cavalry (soldiers on horseback). Oyo power was diminished in the late 1700s, when the Fulani people from the north cut off their supply of horses and took over part of their empire.

The Kingdom of Benin

Farther south on the delta, near the coast, was the kingdom of Benin. This kingdom likely emerged sometime between 800 CE and the 1200s. The height of the Benin kingdom's power spanned from around 1300 to the late 1700s. The Benin capital city, Edo, is the site of modern-day Benin City.

The Benin people had a highly organized government structure, led by their king who was referred to as the Oba. Like the Oni of Ife, the Oba was the physical form of the top god in the Oba religion. The most respected citizens among

This Benin ivory sculpture from the sixteenth century depicts Portuguese noblemen.

the Benin were hunters. Hunting was an elite profession that required a long apprenticeship during which people learned how to survive in the forest for days while tracking game. Most revered were the elephant hunters, who were almost legendary as a result of their bravery. The Benin people were known for their brass and bronze work, made several hundred years ahead of any other West African society.

The Benin encountered the Portuguese in the 1470s and quickly established a good relationship with them. The region was already a center for trade with the rest of Africa because of its location on the Gulf of Guinea, and it soon became a major

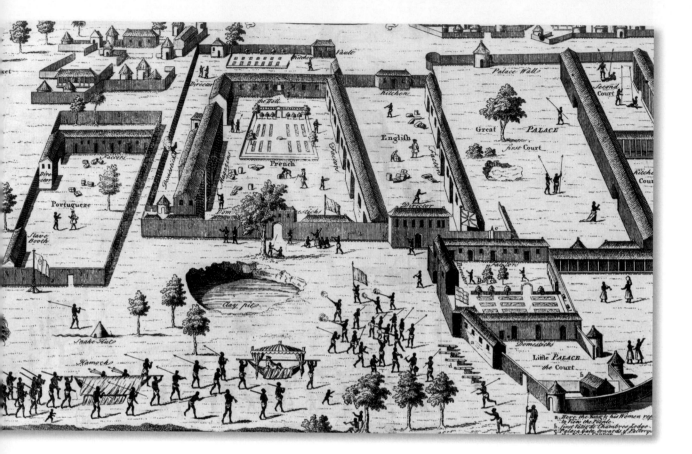

European slave traders built compounds along the coast of the Gulf of Guinea in what is now Nigeria. They imprisoned captive Africans in the compounds until they could be shipped to the Americas.

trade port for Europeans as well. The Benin received products like guns from the Portuguese and silk from the Dutch, and in return traded brass and bronze work, elephant tusks, cotton, and slaves. Benin City would end up being one of the main slave trade ports in West Africa, and this section of the Gulf of Guinea came to be called the Slave Coast.

Exploited by Slavery

The Portuguese began transporting Africans to be used as slaves not long after they sailed down the Gulf of Guinea. When outsiders showed interest in purchasing humans, local traders saw it as a huge financial opportunity. The Benin, as well as their Yoruba and Igbo neighbors, were heavily involved in the slave trade with Europe and eventually the Americas. The slave trade was at its most active during the 1600s, but continued through the 1800s.

African traders got slaves by invading other areas and abducting people. Traders would exchange the prisoners for guns and gunpowder, which they then used to gather more people. In some places, entire communities were taken, while in others, people fled, managing to escape this fate. The popu-

Hundreds of Africans were packed together belowdeck on each slave ship crossing the Atlantic Ocean. In total, between ten and twelve million enslaved Africans were transported to the Americas between the 1500s and the 1800s.

Early Abolitionist

Olaudah Equiano was the youngest son of a judge, and was in training to become one himself. His community, in what is now Nigeria, was referred to as Isseke, or "music and dance people."

One day, while his parents were out working, eleven-year-old Olaudah and his sister were kidnapped by slave traders. After a few days of travel, they were separated, never to see each other again. Olaudah was sold to an African chieftain at first, and then later to traders from overseas. He endured the terrifying journey across the Atlantic Ocean to North America.

He was eventually purchased by a Royal Navy lieutenant named Michael Henry Pascal in the colony of Virginia. Compared to many other enslaved Africans, he was well treated. For seven years he served Pascal. During that time, he traveled to England and was able to educate himself. In 1766, he was able to buy his freedom.

THE

INTERESTING NARRATIVE

OF

THE LIFE

OF

OLAUDAH EQUIANO,

OR

GUSTAVUS VASSA,

THE AFRICAN.

WRITTEN BY HIMSELF.

VOL I.

Behold, God is my salvation; I will trust and not be afraid, for the Lord Jehovah is my strength and my song; he also is become my salvation.
And in that day shall ye say, Praise the Lord, call upon his name, declare his doings among the people. Isaiah xii. 2, 4.

LONDON:

Printed for and sold by the AUTHOR, No. 10, Union-Street, Middlesex Hospital;

Sold also by Mr. Johnson, St. Paul's Church-Yard; Mr. Murray, Fleet-Street; Messrs. Robson and Clark, Bond-Street; Mr. Davis, opposite Gray's Inn, Holborn; Messrs. Shepperson and Reynolds, and Mr. Jackson, Oxford-Street; Mr. Lackington, Chiswell-Street; Mr. Mathews, Strand; Mr. Murray, Prince's-Street, Soho; Mess. Taylor and Co. South Arch, Royal Exchange; Mr. Button, Newington-Causeway; Mr. Parsons, Paternoster-Row; and may be had of all the Booksellers in Town and Country.

[Entered at Stationer's Hall.]

As a free man, Equiano was an abolitionist, or anti-slavery activist. He lectured on the freeing of slaves and actively helped to resettle those who had been freed. In 1766, Equiano wrote his autobiography, *The Interesting Narrative of the Life of Olaudah Equiano, or Gustavus Vassa, the African*. In it, he described his life as a child in Africa and his kidnapping, as well as the cruel way enslaved Africans were treated in the Americas. He hoped that the book would help end slavery.

He argued for the end of slavery to anyone who would listen, including writing letters to the queen of England herself. Equiano died in 1797, just ten years before Britain abolished the slave trade.

lation grew smaller and smaller. The people in some coastal towns became part of the slave trading business as a way to keep from becoming its victims.

By the mid-1700s, Christian missionaries had begun to preach against slavery, and Britain soon stopped trading altogether. In the 1800s, the British Navy sometimes stopped ships full of outbound slaves and brought the captives to other parts of Africa, where they were taught by missionaries. Many of the freed Africans then returned to their homelands, bringing the missionaries to regions where they had not previously been. Because of this, Christianity gained a solid following in the regions that were hit the hardest by the slave trade.

Islam Arrives

While Christianity was taking hold in the southern regions of Nigeria, Islam was taking hold in the north and northwest. It was first introduced to the region in about 1050 CE. Muslim missionaries from Mali, to the northwest, introduced Islam to the Hausa states. Along with Islam, they also promoted literacy (the ability to read and write) and brought in a new legal system. By 1800, the Hausa states had mostly converted to Islam, and their governments had begun to incorporate Islamic law into their own traditional systems.

A Fulani Muslim man named Usman dan Fodio was upset because he believed that the Hausas were mixing Islam with local religious practices. He was a powerful and influential man, and soon had an army of followers who wanted to overthrow the Hausa government. In 1804, he launched a jihad,

After Islam arrived in what is now northern Nigeria, the Hausa people made highly decorated copies of the Qur'an, the Muslim holy book.

or holy war, in order to purify Islam among the Hausas. His cause gained more support as he recruited the masses of poor and oppressed to rise up. By the end of the war, the entire northwest region was united under one religious/political government, called a caliphate. Sokoto, a city in the northwest, served as its headquarters, and Usman dan Fodio's son, Mohammed Bello, was the first sultan, or leader, of what later became known as the Sokoto Caliphate.

Growing British Power

Although the British were not the first Europeans to arrive along the Nigerian coast, they became the primary trading partner of the coastal cities. After they stopped trading slaves, the British began to take an interest in the production of palm oil, which is used in cooking and in many nonfood products such as soaps and makeup. The British were soon buying large quantities of palm oil, which comes from the fruit of oil palm trees.

As other countries such as France began to take an interest in the area's resources, the British became worried that they would lose their advantage in the Niger Delta. In 1886, the Royal Niger Company was formed to oversee trade and administer the Sokoto Caliphate and nearby regions. Then, in 1894, it merged with other British groups in charge of neighboring areas, and the British military moved in to secure British interests. Some local people resisted, fighting to keep control of their land. The Ekumeku movement of Igbos in the southeast were able to hold off the British until 1914, but most of modern-day Nigeria was under British rule by 1905.

The British government renamed the northern region the Northern Nigeria Protectorate, and the southern section of the Niger River including its delta region was named the Southern Nigeria Protectorate and the colony of Lagos. In 1914, these were combined to form the Colony and Protectorate of Nigeria.

The British had complete power over their new colony, but they allowed most day-to-day political functions to remain as they were. As long as the local leaders were cooperative, they were left to rule as they had been. This approach was referred to as "native administration" and was used throughout Britain's African colonies.

British colonial officials pose with a Yoruba king.

The British had a political strategy behind what looked like hands-off rule. Outwardly, it appeared that they were allowing people to live without British control. Yet behind the scenes, the British played a large role. They carefully separated different groups of Nigerians, so they would not join together and revolt against colonial rule. In places without a defined political structure, the British set up local governments using a combination of local and British rulers. They also replaced traditional leaders in areas where there was more resistance to British rule, especially in the north where the Muslim population wanted nothing to do with the Christian rulers.

Changes from the West

British control resulted in many changes. The British created a formal education system, and English became the official language. The British also helped strengthen the infrastructure, increasing the number and quality of roads. Literacy and communication improved. The economy changed as well. The region saw the introduction of cash crops such as cacao, which is used to make chocolate, and palm oil. Paper currency was also introduced. The southern regions of the colony were generally more open to the

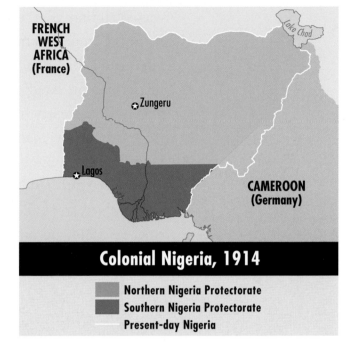

Colonial Nigeria, 1914

- Northern Nigeria Protectorate
- Southern Nigeria Protectorate
- Present-day Nigeria

changes that the British brought. This would give these states advantages over the northern states. These differences caused economic separation between the northern and southern regions and aroused tension.

The British did not always treat their subjects fairly, and the local people resisted regularly. Nigerians were particularly upset when their own soldiers were sent to fight Britain's war in World War I.

Nationalism Swells

During the 1920s, the Pan-Africanism movement gained momentum. This movement focused on ridding the continent of European control and racism. A leader of this movement was Nigerian Herbert Macaulay. He was the grandson of Bishop Samuel Ajayi Crowther, a returned slave who translated the Bible into the Yoruba language and the first African to become an Anglican bishop. Macaulay organized Nigeria's first political party, the Nigerian National Democratic Party. In 1923, a few members of this party were elected to the Legislative Council, a body meant to provide political representation to Nigerians. Macaulay inspired Nigerian nationalism and encouraged people to speak up against British rule. In 1944, he and an Igbo man named Nnamdi Azikiwe

Tens of thousands of Nigerians fought for the British during World War I.

Independence

The British granted Nigeria its independence on October 1, 1960, and exactly three years later Nigeria became a republic, a country where people elect their representatives. Unfortunately, self-rule was a difficult task. The young country needed to figure out how to unify millions of people with differing educational, ethnic, economic, and religious backgrounds. Each of the country's geographic divisions was

Nnamdi Azikiwe was the son of a clerk who worked for the British government. He went to university in the United States before returning to Nigeria and becoming central in the independence movement. He later became the nation's first president.

mainly controlled by that region's ethnic majority. In the north, a Muslim region, the Hausa-Fulanis had most of the power. In the southern part of the country, the Igbos were dominant in the east and the Yorubas in the west. Both parts of the south were primarily Christian.

North and south were at odds constantly, each afraid that the other would gain more power in the federal government and take over. To make things worse, the election system was flawed and corrupt from the beginning, and many leaders were elected unfairly. This did not give anyone faith in the democratic system, and there was a countrywide boycott of the election in 1964. This was the beginning of a period of government turmoil that would last more than thirty years.

In January 1966, a coup led by mostly southern military officers overthrew the government of Prime Minister Abubakar Balewa of the Northern Peoples Congress. He and two other top government figures were murdered. The new head of state was Johnson Aguiyi-Ironsi from the Igbo region. He planned to get rid of all regional government. But just six months into his rule, northern military leaders assassinated him. Yakubu Gowon, who was considered a compromise figure because he was from the central part of the country, took over military rule of Nigeria. The army was split politically, and civil war was beginning.

The War Within

In May 1967, the Igbo-led Eastern region declared itself separate from Nigeria, taking the name the Republic of Biafra. The

governor of this region, Odumegwu Ojukwu, declared himself head of state. People in the Eastern region wanted to break away because they believed that Igbos were persecuted in the Northern region. But the military government, dominated by northerners, did not want to lose the valuable resources found in the East.

Within two months, the conflict had turned into civil war. In August 1967, Biafran troops took over Benin City in the West, and Nigerian troops retaliated with a full attack on Biafra. The rebels did not give up, even though the Nigerian army quickly took the Biafran capital. This war lasted nearly

Nigerian and British officials take part in Nigeria's independence ceremony in 1960.

Biafran soldiers emerge from a trench during the Nigerian Civil War in 1968.

three years, and many people died, both soldiers and civilians. By the official Biafran surrender on January 15, 1970, the population of the eastern states was literally starving. The nation, however, was reunified, and the region was accepted back into the republic.

Oil had been discovered in the Niger Delta in the 1950s, and in the years after the war, the oil industry boomed. Although this gave the government a huge influx of income, the people of Nigeria did not benefit from it. Little was done to help average Nigerians, to improve the country's roads and other infrastructure, or to help the economy grow.

Return to Civilian Rule

Transition back to civilian rule had been promised for 1976, but Yakubu Gowon was not showing any signs of following through. On July 30, 1975, General Murtala Ramat Mohammed overthrew Gowon and immediately began to end military rule. He concentrated on removing corrupt members of the government in order to restore citizens' faith in their government.

He also started the process of making Abuja, a centrally located city, the new capital. He hoped that this would help all parts of the country feel equally represented. He was soon killed, however, and his top aide, Olusegun Obasanjo, took over and continued to prepare the government for the upcoming changes. He created a new constitution that established a presidential system.

The first presidential election was held in 1979. A conservative politician named Shehu Shagari won in a close race. Nigerians soon discovered that their new president was no different from those of the past, taking advantage of government money and abusing his power. Nigerians were angry, yet Shagari won reelection in 1983. His reelection was clearly the result of election fraud, and he was quickly overthrown in a military coup.

Under Military Rule Again

Major General Muhammadu Buhari took leadership of the government. He claimed that he had stepped in to save the country from decline. Buhari introduced a policy he called

War Against Indiscipline (WAI), which prosecuted many of the politicians involved in the recent corruption. At first, the public was happy to see this, but soon Nigerians realized that he was arresting anyone who disagreed with him, including members of the press.

In response, General Ibrahim Babangida staged a coup and took over, promising that he would free those wrongly imprisoned. His official position was that he was working toward establishing civilian leadership. He set 1990 as the year of transition. Behind the scenes, however, Babangida was doing

Muhammadu Buhari had spent most of his career in the military before taking over as head of state following a coup in 1983.

everything he could to keep this from happening. The year 1990 came and went, and when primary elections were held in 1992, he nullified them in an attempt to keep control.

As part of Babangida's "transition" to civilian rule, the government created two new political parties to replace the many that citizens had formed. The National Republican Convention (NRC) represented conservative views, and the Social Democratic Party (SDP) represented liberal views. The parties were told what their agendas would be, and no other parties were allowed. The 1993 presidential elections were held, but Babangida voided the results and the winner never took office.

Voiding the elections led to mass protests across the country. In August 1993, Babangida was forced to step down. A civilian government was briefly in power, but by November General Sani Abacha had taken over as military leader. Like earlier military leaders, he promised that he would soon return power to civilians, but he soon stopped pretending.

Abacha's rule was violent and harsh. He used military force against anyone who opposed him and changed the law to suit his needs. The nation's economy grew, but its people suffered. Abacha and his close circle stole millions of dollars from the government and abused his power while taking personal liberty and basic rights away from citizens. He scheduled an election for 1998 and paid off the political parties to nominate him as the only person running. He died suddenly just before the election. Many think that he was poisoned.

His replacement, General Abdulsalam Abubakar, was in

Nigerians march in favor of a workers' strike in 2004. In the early 2000s, Nigerians held strikes to protest an increase in government-controlled fuel prices. Workers stayed home, forcing schools and businesses to close.

fact eager to turn the government back over to the people. The following year, he freed political prisoners, encouraged free political parties to form, and oversaw successful elections for state and federal positions. He handed over power on May 29, 1999, to the winner of the peaceful election, Olusegun Obasanjo. The nation had civilian rule at last.

Recent Times

In the early 2000s, the Niger Delta's oil industry experienced workers' strikes. There were also attacks on facilities, pipelines, and foreign oil employees. The Movement for the

Emancipation of the Niger Delta (MEND) claimed responsibility for these attacks and demanded more local control of the industry and more benefits from the oil wealth.

By 2008, the nation's focus had turned to the northern states, where the terrorist group Boko Haram was becoming increasingly violent. The violence became so extreme that in 2013, President Goodluck Jonathan declared a state of emergency in three northern states. Although the government has been unable to end the violence, and conflict continues to plague the Nigerian people, the civilian government of Nigeria has maintained its leadership.

Terrorism in Northern Nigeria

Since 2003 northeastern Nigeria has been plagued by an Islamic extremist terrorist group called Boko Haram. The words *boko haram* roughly translate from Hausa to "western education is forbidden." The goal of this group seems to be to create an Islamic state, although they often make other demands and refuse to negotiate.

The group is opposed to girls getting an education, and opposes anything else that it thinks represents the West. Boko Haram made international news in 2011 when a suicide bomber drove his car into the United Nations headquarters in Abuja. In April 2014, they kidnapped 276 girls from a school, most of whom still remain missing. Since that time, numerous attacks have taken place in Borno, Yobe, and Adamawa States, killing or injuring thousands of people.

Since 2014, military forces from Nigeria and other nations have had limited success against Boko Haram. The Nigerian military and law enforcement do not have the resources needed to effectively track and fight the extremists. Military action against Boko Haram has resulted in many deaths. The total number of people killed by both sides is estimated at more than twenty thousand.

Governing a Young Country

CHAPTER 5

NIGERIA IS GOVERNED UNDER A CONSTITUTION THAT was adopted at the end of the last period of military rule. It became effective on May 29, 1999. Like the U.S. government, the Nigerian government is made up of three independent parts: the executive, legislative, and judicial branches.

Although Nigeria has a democratic form of government, the country has faced many challenges because of the continued corruption of government officials, including presidents. The worst abuses of power have been the theft of enormous sums of money from the government. This has left Nigerians with little faith in the democratic system.

Opposite: **A woman in Abuja casts her ballot. Nigerian citizens who are at least eighteen years old can vote.**

A Look at the Capital

The original capital of Nigeria was the large coastal city of Lagos. But in the 1980s, General Murtala Mohammed, the head of state, decided Nigeria needed a capital that could unify Nigerians, so he moved the capital to the center of the country. Construction of a new capital city was started in the town of Abuja. Prior to then, Abuja had been a collection of villages, mostly populated by people who identified as part of the Gwari and Koro ethnic groups.

The capital officially moved to Abuja on December 12, 1991. At the time, Abuja had a population of 107,000. By 2012, the population had grown to more than 2.4 million.

The city is noted for two immense monolithic stone outcrops. The Aso Rock, near the major government buildings, reaches a height of more than 1,200 feet (365 m), and the Zuma Rock, north of town, rises 2,379 feet (725 m). The home of Nigeria's president is called Aso Rock Presidential Villa. Traditionally, the Abuja area was noted for its pottery and agriculture. Today, it is best known for government and business, and there is little tourism. A large, modern downtown district has been developing since 1991, but most areas outside of the city are impoverished.

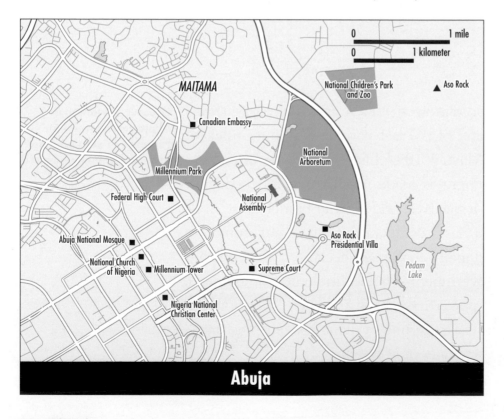

Abuja

Making Laws

Nigeria's legislative branch is called the National Assembly. The National Assembly has two bodies, the Senate and the House of Representatives. Together, these two houses create the laws for governing Nigeria.

The Nigerian Senate has 109 members. Each of Nigeria's thirty-six states elects three senators. The federal capital territory of Abuja has one senator of its own. Senators serve four-year terms. The leader of the Senate is called the president of the Senate. He or she is elected by the members of the Senate from among its members.

The Nigerian Parliament meets in Abuja.

The House of Representatives has 360 members, each chosen by a simple majority in a voting district. Like Senators, House members serve four-year terms. The House's chief officer, called the Speaker of the House, is elected by the members of the House of Representatives.

Nigeria's National Government

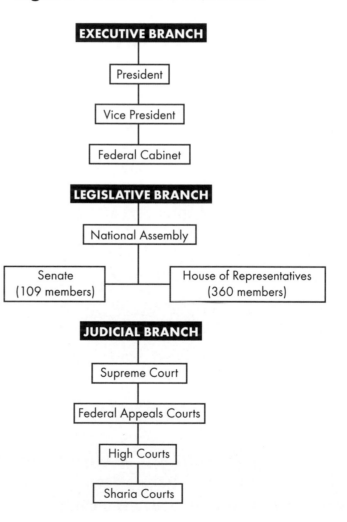

EXECUTIVE BRANCH

President

Vice President

Federal Cabinet

LEGISLATIVE BRANCH

National Assembly

Senate (109 members)

House of Representatives (360 members)

JUDICIAL BRANCH

Supreme Court

Federal Appeals Courts

High Courts

Sharia Courts

Carrying Out Laws

The executive branch is headed by a president and vice president, who are responsible for developing government policies and enforcing laws. In Nigeria, the president is both the head of government, responsible for the operation of the national government, and its head of state, representing the country in foreign affairs and at ceremonies. Nigerians elect the president by a direct vote for a four-year term. The president must receive at least 25 percent of the votes cast in twenty-four of the thirty-six states. In 2015, President Goodluck Jonathan was defeated by retired general Muhammadu Buhari. Oluyemi Osinbajo was elected vice president.

The president appoints ministers to the Federal Cabinet. Each minister is in charge of a different area of government, such as agriculture, education, and finance.

Muhammadu Buhari talks to reporters in 2015, after defeating President Goodluck Jonathan in the presidential election. It was the first time in Nigerian history that a sitting president lost a reelection bid.

Interpreting the Laws

The judicial branch is made up of courts, where cases are tried and laws are interpreted. The Supreme Court is the highest court in the land. It is headed by a chief justice and has fifteen associate judges. The justices are selected by the president from a list of recommendations made by the National Judicial Council. The Supreme Court is responsible for interpreting the laws of the country and for making a final decision in cases that are appealed from lower courts. Nigeria has several federal appeals courts, and there are high courts in each state, where trials are held.

The legal system of Nigeria is a mixture of English common law developed during the colonial period and traditional laws of the local peoples. In the twelve northern states, Islamic law, known as Sharia law, is also in effect.

Islamic Law

Sharia law, or Islamic law, is practiced in twelve of Nigeria's states. Nine of these follow Sharia law at both the civil and criminal levels, while three apply it only in civil cases. A few other countries around the world also follow Sharia law, including Pakistan, Iran, and Saudi Arabia. Under Sharia, some activities are illegal in some places but not in others.

Sharia law is controversial in Nigeria. Although Sharia law is supposed to apply only to Muslims, this is not always the case. In some states all women, including Christians, have been barred from taking part in sports.

Supporters of this law believe that the strict laws and harsh consequences are necessary to curb crime. The laws are based on the concept that the needs of society as a whole are more important than the wants of individuals.

Opponents of Sharia believe that the laws are too extreme and the punishments too severe. They also dislike Sharia because it diminishes the notion of individual rights and freedoms.

States and Local Government

Like the United States, Nigeria is divided into states. The nation has thirty-six states, plus the capital city, Abuja, which is called the federal capital territory. Like the nation as a whole, each state is governed by an executive, a legislative

In 2012, Aloma Mariam Mukhtar became Nigeria's first female Supreme Court chief justice.

National Anthem

The music for the Nigerian national anthem, "Arise, O Compatriots," was written by Benedict Elide Odiase. The lyrics are drawn from the top five entries in a national contest. They were written by John A. Ilechukwu, Eme Etim Akpan, B. A. Ogunnaike, Sota Omoigui, and P. O. Aderibigbe. The anthem was adopted in 1978.

Arise, O compatriots, Nigeria's call obey
To serve our fatherland
With love and strength and faith
The labour of our heroes past
Shall never be in vain
To serve with heart and might
One nation bound in freedom, peace and unity.

Oh God of creation, direct our noble cause
Guide our leader's right
Help our youth the truth to know
In love and honesty to grow
And living just and true
Great lofty heights attain
To build a nation where peace and justice shall reign.

The flag of Nigeria is composed of three vertical bands of color—green on the edges and white in the middle. The green represents the forests and natural resources of Nigeria, while the white represents the national desire for peace and unity. The flag was adopted on October 1, 1960, the day that Nigeria became independent from Great Britain. A contest had been held to design the new flag. The winner was a student, Michael Akinkunmi.

body, and a judicial system. In each state, the enforcement of laws is the responsibility of the governor, the head of the executive branch. Each governor is elected by the voters of the state to a four-year term.

The State House of Assembly is the legislative branch of state government. Each state also has a judicial system that operates like the federal system. State court rulings can be appealed to national courts.

Each state in Nigeria is subdivided into local government areas (LGA). In 2015, there were a total of 774 LGAs in Nigeria. Each LGA is run by a local government council, which is led by a chief executive. Local government is responsible for caring for the poor, maintaining cemeteries, establishing and maintaining markets, and building and maintaining local roads, drainage systems, and parks. LGAs also oversee the registration of births, deaths, and marriages.

CHAPTER 6

Oil and More

BECAUSE OF ITS RICH OIL RESERVES IN THE NIGER Delta, Nigeria has the largest national economy in Africa. Unfortunately, this doesn't help most Nigerians. Almost two-thirds of Nigerians live in extreme poverty, surviving on the equivalent of one dollar a day. About one in three children between the ages of five and fourteen work. Some are working to support their families, but most have been forced to work. They do difficult and dangerous labor like mining, construction, and working on tobacco or cocoa plantations.

Terrorism, unemployment, government corruption, and extremely uneven wealth distribution contribute to Nigeria's economic problems. The nation's large population and high rates of diseases like AIDS also strain the nation's financial stability.

Opposite: **A worker inspects equipment on an oil-drilling platform in Nigeria. Nigeria is the largest oil producer in Africa and the thirteenth-largest in the world.**

Buying and Selling

Nigeria exported about US$51 billion worth of goods in 2015, and 95 percent of that came from the sale of oil, the source of gasoline and many other products. Nigeria also exports large amounts of rubber and cocoa beans. The oil industry supplies the federal government with most of its money, in the form of taxes and fees that the oil companies must pay. The countries that purchase the most Nigerian oil are India, Brazil, the United States, and the European Union. South Africa is the only African country that Nigeria trades with regularly.

The harbor in Lagos. Cranes are used to load huge containers—some the size of a semi truck—onto cargo ships.

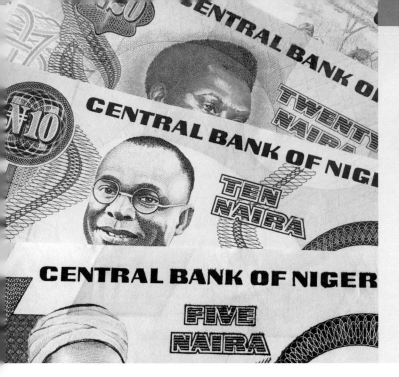

Nigeria imported approximately US$48 billion worth of goods in 2015. More than one-quarter of that total came from China. Vehicles and textiles (fabric) are major imports, as are chemicals, food, and paper products.

From the Earth

Oil is Nigeria's most valuable natural resource. It was first discovered in 1956 in the Niger Delta region. This region holds most of the country's reserves, but reserves have also been found offshore, under the waters in the Gulf of Guinea.

Nigerian oil production is estimated at around 2.5 million barrels a day—that's more than 105 million gallons (400 million liters) each day! Nigeria ranks as the world's twelfth-largest crude oil producer. It exports approximately 2.3 million barrels each day, making it the fifth-largest oil exporter in the world.

A woman lays out clothes to dry on an oil pipeline in the delta region.

Nigeria has four refineries, where crude oil is turned into usable forms, but the nation cannot process as much oil as it needs, so Nigeria actually imports oil. Most oil tankers come and go from the ports at Burutu and Bonny.

Natural gas is another very valuable resource that is abundant in Nigeria. It can be found on its own, but is also a major by-product of the oil industry. In the past, the natural gas that was released from the ground during oil drilling was burned off. More recently, its value has been recognized, and it is being collected as a fuel source. Nigeria's natural gas reserves are large, estimated to be over 5 trillion cubic meters in 2014. Although there is a lot of potential, there is a challenge in transporting the gas. Pipelines are expensive to build and maintain, and vulnerable to accidents.

Coal is also mined in Nigeria. It was first discovered in 1909, and the bulk of the nation's coal mines were established in the Enugu, Kogi, and Anambra states in southern Nigeria. Although many of the nation's mines have shut down, extensive reserves remain, and the mines still supply coal to power plants, railroads, and the metals industry.

Before coal and oil were discovered, Nigeria's major natural resources included tin and iron. Tin and columbite, a mineral source of iron, were mined in the Jos Plateau. This industry saw its peak in the 1950s and 1960s before the oil industry took over. Today, there are over a thousand abandoned mines in the plateau region.

Manufacturing

In Nigeria, manufacturing makes up about one-quarter of the economy and employs 10 percent of the workforce. Nigeria has mills that process raw materials that are unearthed in its mines. There are mills to make steel for domestic use and export. Nigeria also has an aluminum industry.

But many parts of the Nigerian manufacturing industry rely heavily on imported materials, which cuts into profits. At one point the government tried banning imports to boost the

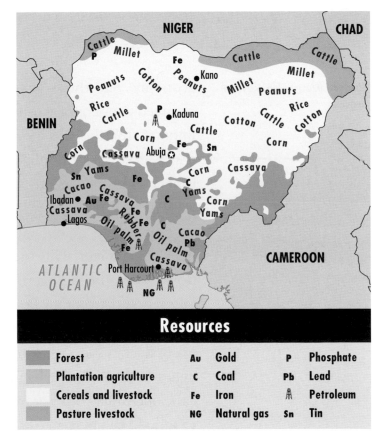

Women weave baskets in Lagos.

economy, but those laws were unworkable and were soon changed to encourage using local resources while still allowing imports. Textiles and shoes, petrochemicals, cement, fertilizer, and paper industries all rely heavily on outside sources. The rubber industry has an advantage because rubber trees grow locally.

Small-scale manufacturing by individuals or families can help them meet daily needs. Their materials usually come from local sources. Nigeria has many ironworkers who produce rakes, hoes, and other farm tools, as well as hardware. Potters create bowls and other containers for everyday use. They also make decorative pieces to sell to tourists. Woodcarving produces both useful items and beautiful crafts. In areas where cane and raffia palms grow, some women weave bags and mats to sell. They also make cane baskets and furniture.

What Nigeria Grows, Makes, and Mines

AGRICULTURE

Cassava (2012)	54,000,000 metric tons
Yams (2012)	38,000,000 metric tons
Goats (2013)	58,250,000 animals

MANUFACTURING (VALUE ADDED, 2012)

Refined petroleum	80,136,000,000 Nigerian naira
Cement	30,214,000,000 Nigerian naira

MINING

Crude oil (2013)	845,000,000 barrels
Natural gas (2011)	38,343,000,000 cubic meters
Limestone (2012)	11,000,000 metric tons

Feeding Many

Although 70 percent of Nigeria's workforce is employed in agriculture, farming accounts for only about one-fifth of the nation's income. This is because most of the farms are small family farms that produce only enough for the family with perhaps a little left over to sell or trade. Nigeria's northern and southern regions have different climates and types of soil, so different crops are grown in each area. The north and south trade their products. The north trades crops like onions and beans to the south in exchange for fruit, plantains, cassava, and nuts. The central region trades yams with its neighbors.

Despite the best efforts of Nigerian farmers, they cannot produce enough food to feed everyone in the country. The soil

Slash and Burn

Some Nigerian farmers clear land using a technique called slash and burn. It involves cutting down all of the plants and trees in the area that will be farmed, and then burning it all. This process helps farmers clear the area where they want to plant, and the ashes fertilize the soil. Unfortunately, slash-and-burn agriculture is bad for the land. Forests are cut, destroying the habitats of many animals. In addition, without plant roots to hold the fertile topsoil in place, it is easily blown or washed away.

quality is poor, and the land has to be worked by hand rather than by machine. Especially in the dry north and other areas far from rivers, getting water to the crops is a major problem. Even places with streams and rivers nearby suffer during the dry season. And some places that were once major irrigation sources, like Lake Chad, are now so overused that farmers cannot get enough water from them.

Despite all of the factors that work against them, Nigerian farmers grow a large variety of products. Staple food crops like rice, corn, millet, cassava, sorghum, and yams are grown mostly for domestic use. Crops like cotton, peanuts, and cacao are used locally and also exported. The government encourages farmers to grow tree products such as rubber, palm oil, and teakwood for industrial uses. Although agricultural exports do not make up a large part of the country's overall income, they are important to the communities that rely on that money for survival.

Livestock is also an important part of agricultural life in Nigeria, especially in the north. The Fulanis raise cattle, mainly to make dairy products. They also trade beef and hides with southern farmers for fruits and vegetables. Nigerians raise goats for both meat and dairy products, while pigs and sheep are bred for their meat and hides. Fish from the Gulf of Guinea, as well as lakes, reservoirs, and seasonal pools, are eaten by locals but not exported.

Service Industries

Services, which include government jobs, health care, teaching, and sales, make up a little more than half of Nigeria's economy, and employ 20 percent of the workforce. Despite Nigeria's rich cultures, tourism is almost nonexistent. The

Cattle drink at a well in northern Nigeria. There are about twenty million head of cattle in the country.

Most roads in Nigeria are unpaved.

threat of violence keeps visitors away. For years, military rule made travel unpredictable, and now religious and ethnic conflicts make it dangerous. In addition, ethnic conflict and the threat of terrorism keep many would-be foreign investors from getting involved in business in Nigeria.

Transportation Trouble

Over the years in Nigeria, many officials have taken government money for themselves rather than using it for what it was intended. As a result, the country has a poor infrastructure, which holds back its economic progress. Only 15 percent of the nation's 120,000 miles (193,000 km) of roads are paved, and no roads are well maintained. Travel by car or bus is difficult, and traffic jams are constant in the cities. Most Nigerians cannot afford a vehicle of their own, so it is common to see pickup

trucks loaded with people on their way to work. Trains are unreliable and rarely used for passenger travel.

Inland water travel is often difficult as well, despite Nigeria's many rivers. The Niger is broken up by frequent sections of rocky rapids and waterfalls, and many smaller waterways dry up easily and are not dependable for transportation. The Benue River is the only inland waterway that is used regularly to transport people and goods.

Economic growth is also held back by a lack of dependable electricity. The demand for power is much greater than the current system can produce, even though the country has vast reserves of coal, natural gas, and oil. The fuel has been exported rather than being turned into electricity for people at home. As a result, many Nigerian families do not have any electricity in homes, and many businesses suffer frequent power loss.

Nigeria has two major international ports, Lagos and Port Harcourt, as well as many smaller seaports. Pirates are active, however, along the Gulf of Guinea coast, and the armed robbery of cargo ships discourages sea trade.

A farmer plows a field in the fertile land of southern Nigeria.

A Struggling Economy

Nigeria's rich natural resources should mean a prosperous economy, yet the majority of its residents live in extreme poverty.

For a nation's economy to work, all of its parts need to work together. Hundreds of different ethnic groups are found within the political borders that were set during British rule, and some of them have been at odds for centuries. Religious differences create conflict between the north and south. In addition, the north is at an economic disadvantage because in the south, both oil and land are better suited for agriculture.

The instability of the government has made these problems even worse. Both military and civilian leaders have stolen enormous amounts of money from the government, leaving almost nothing for the nation. Even though this has

Many Nigerians sell produce such as tomatoes and peppers at markets.

gotten better in recent years, fraud is still common among politicians and large sums of money often go missing.

Poor organization of the government also keeps the various industries and regions from working together, and the economy suffers. There is a lot of power at the top, and little at the local level. Economic regulations change often, reform in the legislature is slow, and laws are not enforced. Because of this, a few very wealthy and powerful people can control most of the country's money, while the rest work but see none of it. There is no easy fix for these many problems, but change is possible, and many Nigerians are working to improve their country's economy.

CHAPTER 7

A Diverse Nation

IN 2015, NIGERIA WAS HOME TO AN ESTIMATED 181,562,056 people. This is the highest population of any African nation. About half of the people in Nigeria live in or around cities, while the other half lives in rural areas. The most densely populated areas are along the gulf coast, in the southwest, and the far north. Fewer people live in the central plateau region. Over the past fifty years, there has been extensive migration from rural areas into cities, especially in placcs where the agriculture is poor. There has also been migration from the north to the south because of the violence in the north.

Opposite: **The population of Nigerian cities such as Kano has increased quickly in recent years.**

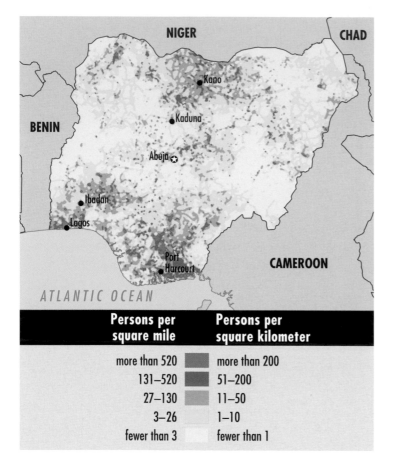

NIGER

CHAD

BENIN

Kano

Kaduna

Abuja ✪

Ibadan

Lagos

Port Harcourt

CAMEROON

ATLANTIC OCEAN

Persons per square mile		Persons per square kilometer
more than 520		more than 200
131–520		51–200
27–130		11–50
3–26		1–10
fewer than 3		fewer than 1

Population of Largest Cities (2015 est.)

Lagos	13,123,000
Kano	3,587,000
Ibadan	3,160,000
Abuja	2,440,000
Port Harcourt	2,343,000

Health

On average, each woman in Nigeria gives birth to more than five children. Even though many Nigerian children die from disease when they are quite young, 43 percent of the country's residents are age fourteen and under.

For the majority of Nigerians, the daily quality of life is far worse than low-income families in the United States. Almost one-third of the population does not have access to clean drinking water, and in many areas the family's water supply is a river or creek that is also used for bathing and waste disposal. Only 33 percent of people in cities have any kind of toilet facilities. Sanitation in rural areas is even worse.

Nigerians also have a high risk of infectious diseases. These are spread by contact with infected food, water, insects, animals, other humans, or the air or soil. Common diseases spread in food and water are hepatitis A and typhoid fever. People contract Lassa fever from dust or soil, and insects like mosquitoes transmit malaria, yellow fever, and dengue fever. Since nutrition is poor in many areas, with 31 percent of chil-

Age Distribution

Age	In Nigeria	In United States
0–14	43%	19%
15–24	19%	14%
25–54	31%	40%
55–64	4%	13%
65 & up	3%	14%

dren under age five underweight, their bodies have a harder time fighting off disease and many children die.

A family rides through Akure, in southwestern Nigeria.

HIV is Nigeria's biggest health crisis. It is the virus that causes AIDS, a disease that keeps a person's body from being able to fight off even the smallest infection. In 2014, 3,391,600 Nigerians had AIDS, which is 3 percent of the population, including children. Annually, about 174,000 people die from AIDS-related illnesses. Nigeria's AIDS death rate is

A health care worker in Lagos examines a child. Nearly a third of children in Nigeria do not get enough food to eat.

higher than that of any other country in the world. This puts an enormous burden on individuals and the nation as a whole.

Lack of clean water, lack of access to health care, and widespread infectious diseases all contribute to a high death rate among Nigerians. The life expectancy of the average Nigerian is fifty-three years.

Many Cultures

Nigeria has over 250 ethnic groups. The largest are the Hausas, Fulanis, Yorubas, and Igbos. The Hausa people are most often grouped with the Fulanis because the two groups have shared the same region for several hundred years. Combined, the Hausa-Fulanis make up 29 percent of the total population. The Yorubas occupy a smaller physical area but make up 21 percent of the population. The Igbos account for about 18 percent of the population. Other major ethnic groups include the Ijaws, Kanuris, Ibibios, and Tivs.

There are around forty million Hausas in Nigeria, concentrated in the northern region. Hausas also live in other West African countries, and it is estimated that around 35 million people speak Hausa as a first language.

In northern Nigeria, a large portion of the media is in the Hausa language. Most Hausas live in rural areas, although the city of Kano was founded by the Hausas. Families usually live in small groups that form a compound, which is led by a ruler called the emir. The Hausas are known for their leatherwork and other handcrafts such as weaving.

The Fulanis were the first group in West Africa to convert

Ethnic Groups	
Hausa-Fulani	29%
Yoruba	21%
Igbo	18%
Ijaw	10%
Kanuri	4%
Ibibio	3.5%
Tiv	2.5%

A Fulani boy herds cows. Fulanis measure people's wealth by the number of cows they own.

to Islam. Historically, they were a nomadic cattle-herding people, and cattle remain an important part of their culture and economy. The Fulanis have become intermingled with the Hausas in northern Nigeria. Although they have their own language, Fulfulde, many Fulanis now speak Hausa instead. Traditional Fulani crafts include basket weaving, knitting, and textile weaving. Music is an especially important part of their culture, and the Fulanis have a great appreciation for personal beauty.

The Yoruba people in the southwest, known informally as Yorubaland, make up a little more than one-fifth of Nigeria's population. The borders of their cultural group extend to the west into the country of Benin. Historically, the Yoruba peo-

A Yoruba woman and her children. On average, women in Nigeria have five children.

ple were among the hardest hit by the slave trade. In Nigeria, they have held tight to their traditions and many practice traditional religions along with Christianity. Because of the slave trade, their language and culture have spread to many other parts of the world, especially Brazil, Cuba, and Trinidad and Tobago.

Igboland is the unofficial name for the southeastern area of Nigeria where the Igbos are the largest ethnic group. The Igbos have a strong ethnic identity. Individual groups within the Igbo ethnic group have a wide variety of customs. The Igbos are known for their love of music, their various drums, and their elaborate masks. The rainforest region where they live is ideal for growing root vegetables, and yams are their staple food. Yams are so important that every year at harvest time, they hold a traditional yam festival.

The Igbos are known for placing a high value on education. As a result, they have a higher literacy rate than other Nigerians. Christianity is widespread among the Igbos, but in many areas, people's beliefs are a mixture of Christian and traditional practices.

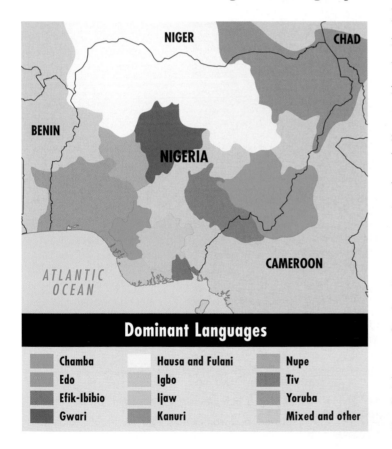

Dominant Languages

	Chamba		Hausa and Fulani		Nupe
	Edo		Igbo		Tiv
	Efik-Ibibio		Ijaw		Yoruba
	Gwari		Kanuri		Mixed and other

How Do You Say . . . ?

English	Yoruba	Igbo	Hausa
Good morning	*Ekuojumo*	*Igbolachi*	*Ina kwana*
Good night	*Odaaro*	*Kachifo*	*Said a safe*
How are you?	*Se daadaa ni?*	*Kedu ka idi?*	*Kana Lafiya?*
Thank you	*E se*	*Dalu*	*Nagode*

A Land of Many Tongues

The official language of Nigeria is English. Along with the Hausa, Fulani, Igbo, and Yoruba languages, more than five hundred other languages are spoken among smaller ethnic groups that are scattered throughout the country.

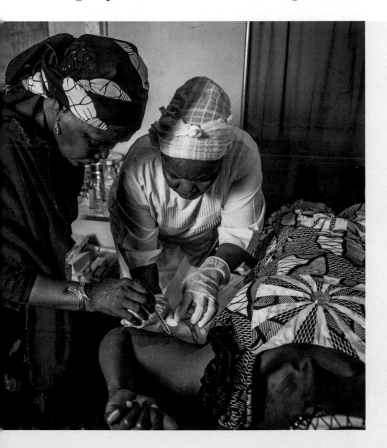

Women in Nigeria

Historically, women have had the jobs of food preparation, making items for daily use like pottery, baskets, and mats, and being in charge of the younger children. This also meant that they had control over household operations and resources, which gave them considerable influence. In precolonial times, women were leaders and held positions with titles and power. The Yorubas honored female chiefs, called *iyalode*.

After the British occupied Nigeria, Western notions about women's roles took over. While the men were turned into soldiers and laborers, the women became responsible for farming to meet the basic needs of the family. A formal education system was introduced, but women and girls were not taught the same subjects and did not end up with the same opportunities as men. Since independence, education for women has improved, and women now hold important roles in government, science, and other academic areas.

CHAPTER 8

Spiritual Life

THE PEOPLE OF NIGERIA FOLLOWED MANY DIFFERENT spiritual belief systems before Christianity and Islam arrived in the area. The practices varied by region and ethnic group. Today in Nigeria, elements of the traditional religions are mixed with Christianity and Islam, especially in the south. About 49 percent of the population identifies as Muslim, followers of the religion of Islam. Another 49 percent consider themselves Christian. The remaining 2 percent are found mostly in isolated rural areas, where they practice their traditional religion.

Opposite: **A woman prays at a mosque in Lagos.**

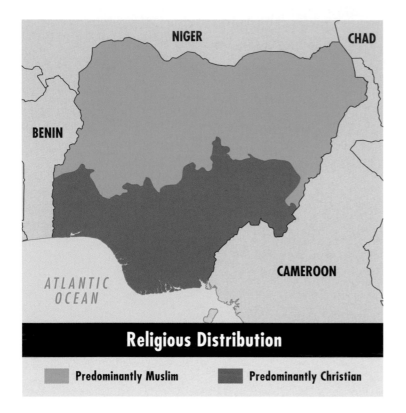

Religious Distribution

Predominantly Muslim   Predominantly Christian

Traditional religions in Nigeria hold many different beliefs and customs, but have some common elements too. They are polytheistic, meaning they recognize multiple gods, also known as deities. Traditional religions place a great deal of importance on the deities' power over weather, crops, livestock, and health. Sacrifices are sometimes made in hopes of earning the good favor of the deities.

Igbo Practices

Even though most Igbo practice some form of Christianity, many also practice traditional beliefs. The Igbo creator god is called Chineke (or Chukwu), and the goddess of the earth is named Ala. There are many other lesser deities who are responsible for different aspects of life and the spiritual world beyond. The Igbos believe in reincarnation, the idea that a person's spirit leaves the body at death and then returns again in a new life. Priests, called *dibia*, have different functions. They are healers, who are said to both intervene with the spirits and use herbs to cure illness. Divining (fortune-telling) is one of their most important rituals. Both male and female spiritual leaders are highly respected.

Yoruba Practices

Like the Igbos, the Yorubas have incorporated their traditional religion into Christian worship. There are more than four hundred gods and goddesses in the traditional Yoruba religion, each with specific responsibilities and their own set of rituals and requirements. The top deity is called Olorun (meaning "owner of heaven"). Another deity, Eshu, acts as a messenger. He brings sacrifices to the supreme god and delivers Olorun's messages to humans.

The Yorubas believe that the conscious spiritual state of an individual, called *ori* (head), is more important than the rituals of specific religious practices. They believe that the goal of the *ori-inu* (spiritual awareness in the physical human

The Osun River is sacred to the Yoruba people. Every year, thousands of people bathe in the river during a festival honoring the river goddess.

Catholic Nigerians pray at a church in Kano. Catholics are the largest Christian group in Nigeria.

body) is to improve their character, or *Iwa*. In between physical lives, the spirit becomes one with the *Olodumare*, which is part of Olorun. The spirit is then reincarnated, most often into a descendant. Names of children are often chosen based on this belief.

Christianity

European traders first brought Christianity to Nigeria. The religion was later spread by missionaries. Christianity was particularly appealing to those who were trying to fight the slave trade because it emphasized the value of individuals. The religion spread rapidly in the areas that suffered the most from the slave trade, which were the places most accessible to the coast, in the south.

There are many different forms of Christianity, including the Roman Catholic Church, various Protestant churches, and others like the Unitarian Church. The details of these faiths vary, but they are all based on the teachings of Jesus in the New Testament and the doctrine of the Old Testament of the Bible. A wide variety of Christian religions are represented in Nigeria. The most common are Roman Catholic, Anglican, Methodist, and Baptist. Many Nigerians also belong to Pentecostal churches, which emphasize a direct experience of God. These include the Redeemed Christian Church of God and the Christ Apostolic Church. Most Nigerians incorporate parts of their traditional beliefs into their Christian worship, and some churches include drumming and dancing in their services.

Islam

Islam arrived in what is now Nigeria from the north in about 1050. By the 1800s, it had become the dominant religion among the Hausas.

Like Christianity, Islam has different sects, or groups. In Islam there are just two major sects, Sunni and Shia. In Nigeria, the majority of Muslims are Sunni. A minority of Shia live mostly in the Kaduna region in northwestern Nigeria. It is much less common for Muslim Nigerians to incorporate parts of traditional religions into their worship, although a small number known as the Maguzawas, a subgroup of the Hausas, still practice their ancestral beliefs.

Nigerian Sunnis belong to the Maliki school or branch of Islam. This groups feels strongly about the need for Sharia,

Nigerian Muslims show their joy during Eid al-Fitr. In Nigeria, people celebrate the end of Ramadan with a festive meal.

or Islamic law. Although freedom of religion is guaranteed in the Nigerian constitution, which also prohibits states from declaring an official or mandatory religion, Muslims in northern Nigeria have imposed Sharia law in twelve states. This is a major source of friction between Islamic groups and the federal government.

Like Muslims around the world, Nigerian Muslims pray five times a day. The holiest time of year is Ramadan, the ninth month of the Islamic calendar. This is the month during which Muhammad, the prophet of Islam, is said to have first received messages from God. Ramadan is a time of renewed devotion and reflection. During the entire month, Muslims fast—do not eat—during daylight hours. This helps them focus their thoughts on spiritual matters, improve self-control, and increase sympathy for people who have nothing. At the end of the month is a festival called Eid al-Fitr, during which people feast with family and friends.

Religious Conflict

The origins and some of the basic teachings of Islam and Christianity are similar. Both are monotheistic (believe in only one god) and consider the Ten Commandments to be the ultimate law as presented by the prophet Moses. Muslims do not believe that Jesus was literally the son of god, but respect his teachings as a prophet just as much as Christians do. In contrast, Muslims do not feel that saints should be prayed to in the way that many Catholics do, and they do not believe that humans are born into the world as sinners.

Even though they are only a very tiny percentage of Muslims, extremist groups like Boko Haram are opposed to Christianity to the point of violence. In Nigeria, conflicts between Muslims and Christians overlap with disagreements between ethnic groups that have been at odds since long before formalized religion came to West Africa. Outsiders sometimes assume that the violence that erupts is about religious

differences. In reality, the people committing violent attacks have a variety of motivations, including political ambition, financial gain, and pure anger over the conditions of their homeland. Many of the Boko Haram recruits are young people with few options who are easily drawn to a cause that promises a better life.

The majority of Muslims and Christians get along well in Nigeria and the rest of the world. In regions like Yorubaland, they live and work side by side free of conflict.

CHAPTER 9

A Vibrant Culture

THE MUSIC TRADITIONS OF THE YORUBA PEOPLE HAVE had a big influence on Nigeria's modern popular music. Ancient Yoruba music relied on drums, but from the earliest contact with Europeans and other traders, the Yorubas adopted other influences into their music. These included adding brass instruments, incorporating drumming styles brought by Islamic merchants, and taking up Brazilian beats introduced by the Portuguese.

Opposite: **Yoruba drummers perform at a festival.**

Nigerian Music

These various influences came together in the port of Lagos and other cities where people of different cultures lived, and they form the roots of Nigerian music today. This has devel-

Talking Drums

The double-ended talking drum, one of the oldest traditional instruments used by the Yoruba and Hausa people of Nigeria, gets its name from the way it can imitate human speech. The two drumheads (the flexible coverings that the drummer hits with his hands) are connected along the outside of the drum by tight leather cords, so that as the player squeezes the drum between the arm and body, the sound changes. The drum is not easy to play, but a skilled player can learn to "speak" whole phrases with it. Talking drums were used to communicate, sometimes to send secret messages between villages in times of war and other times as a different way of reciting poetry. The Yorubas and other West African people developed a special vocabulary of drum language, and the skills were passed down in the same family.

oped into distinct musical forms, known as *waka*, *sakara*, and *fuji*, all of which are influenced by Islamic music but are based firmly in Yoruba musical traditions and sung in the Yoruba language. Often even international styles such as rap use the Yoruba language in Nigeria. Traditionally, Yoruba music is spiritual and reflects religious beliefs.

The Nigerian music style the world knows best is Afrobeat, which is popular throughout all of West Africa. It has a lively beat. Like Yoruba music, Afrobeat is not entirely African, as it incorporates elements from jazz, funk, soul, and other styles.

Nigeria's most famous musician, Fela Kuti, is credited with originating Afrobeat and is certainly its best-known performer. Soon after he began performing in 1961, he was influenced by other African musicians, and together they developed this distinctive style. Fela Kuti visited the United States in the 1960s, and was greatly influenced by the American civil rights movement. He often wound political themes into his music, singing against corruption and police abuses. Two of his children, Femi Kuti and Seun Kuti, are popular Afrobeat musicians.

Another popular musical style among the Yorubas is called *juju*. It uses guitars and talking drums, mixing traditional Yoruba

Afrobeat musician Fela Kuti was the son of women's right activist Funmilayo Ransome-Kuti.

A musician in Katsina, in northern Nigeria, plays a traditional flute.

music with rock and roll. King Sunny Ade is a leading juju musician who has influenced other musicians around the world.

Children's Music

Nigerian children, like those in other countries, have songs and singing games of their own. Many of these involve one child singing a line and the rest responding in a chorus. Very often these songs use old-fashioned forms of the language that are no longer used in everyday speech.

Children also play homemade musical instruments, including drums made from tin cans and pipes made from the hollow stems of the pawpaw plant. They make a type of mouth harp from the stalks of sorghum, a plant grown for sugar. Another is a stringed instrument similar to a zither, made from cornstalks.

The most unusual instrument is played by Hausa children—a drum made from the inflated stomach of a pufferfish.

Sculptures in Brass and Clay

Art traditions are similar among many West African people, but some groups have particular specialties. For example, the Yorubas are renowned for their brass sculpture. Using a method called lost wax, an artist begins by carving a detailed sculpture in beeswax. This is then covered in clay, leaving a stem of wax. When the clay hardens, the wax is melted and

A Nigerian bronze caster carefully carves a figure.

This miniature Yoruba head is from an ancestral shrine.

runs out through the hole left by the stem. Then the empty mold is filled with molten (melted) brass and allowed to cool. When the clay mold is broken away, the result is an exact brass replica of the wax model, perfect in every detail. Because the mold is broken, each casting is an original work of art. Although these works are usually in brass, they are sometimes known as Benin bronzes. Some of the world's finest brass sculpture is Yoruba work.

Before brass was available, the ancient Nok people were making magnificent sculptures in terra-cotta, a type of clay that is worked while soft and then dried and baked to make it hard. Beautifully detailed Nok terra-cotta sculptures have been found that date from as early as 500 BCE.

Faces and Figures

The Yorubas and other peoples of Nigeria have been skilled woodcarvers since ancient times. Woodcarving was traditionally done with iron tools made by local blacksmiths. Detailed masks and figures were originally painted, but on most of the objects found in museums, the paint has worn off. Carved wooden masks were used in funerals to represent the spirits of the departed. Other masks were humorous and were used in parades and festivals.

Egungun (Yoruba) and Mmanwu (Igbo) masks were worn by men in secret religious societies. Some of these masks covered the entire head, and even those that didn't, disguised the wearer completely. It was important to keep the members' identities secret. The details of the masks are different in each culture. Experts can tell what culture a sculpture comes from by details such as the shape of the ears or the way teeth are shown.

Many Nigerian groups use traditionally carved wooden masks. This one was made by people of the Idoma culture.

In Kano, artisans dye cloth in dye pits.

Yoruba arts also include fabric weaving, basket and mat weaving, tie-dyeing, beadwork, appliqué in cloth and leather, and carving gourds, stone, wood, and ivory. The arts of the Igbo people are similar to those of the Yorubas, but the Igbo also carve drums, stools, and doorways. Some Igbo groups decorate their houses with painted wall murals.

Nigerian Art in a Modern World

Sculpture and other artistic traditions have survived better in Nigeria than in other parts of West Africa, because during the colonial era British leaders in Nigeria took an active role in protecting and preserving local arts and studying their history. There was also little attempt to stamp out local customs. This was in sharp contrast to the attitudes of Belgian, French, and other colonial powers elsewhere in Africa.

Many traditional woodcarvings were used in religious ceremonies. Although African religions survived European contact and are still strong even today, they were constantly changing. These shifting practices affected artists, because as old ceremonies became less important, artists lost much of their market for selling masks and other carvings used in ceremonial activities. But as this was happening, new markets opened up as a result of the increased interest in African art by collectors and museums. The best work of skilled Nigerian artists is highly prized by collectors today.

The Igbo people make elaborate masks for their ceremonies. This mask, representing a hippopotamus, was used during a festival honoring water spirits.

The National Museum

The Nigerian National Museum in Lagos displays some of the finest examples of Nigerian art found anywhere, including sculptures in brass, wood, and terra-cotta. It also has exhibits on the Nok and other early peoples, revealing what is known about their way of life.

The museum was founded in 1957 by the English archaeologist Kenneth Murray, who served as Director of the Department of Antiquities. It was Murray's dedication to protecting Nigeria's art that convinced the British colonial authorities to take steps to collect it and preserve it from looting as ancient sites were discovered. Before his intervention, many precious works were taken out of Nigeria and sold to private collectors and museums. Even today, Nigeria is trying to get some of these returned to be shown in the National Museum.

African sculpture had a great influence on modern Western art by freeing artists from the idea that everything they created had to look exactly as it did in real life. African traditions didn't limit artists to showing everything as it actually looks, and when European artists saw the beauty of African art, they began to think in terms of more abstract figures. African sculptures inspired the great Spanish artist Pablo Picasso to experiment with his abstract style called cubism, which began the entire modern art movement.

The Yoruba people's cultural influences were felt in other parts of the world as well. Because a great many people who were taken to the Americas as slaves in the sixteenth to the nineteenth centuries were from Yoruba regions, the group's cultural influences were strong in Brazil, Cuba, and the United States, even showing up in the language.

Nigerian peoples have a long heritage of storytelling, not only as entertainment but as a way to pass history, religious

A woodcarver transforms a log into a life-size figure.

In his books, Ben Okri explores the politics and culture of Nigeria.

beliefs, and traditions from one generation to the next. Proverbs are a common way to share wisdom by explaining things in symbols that everyone can understand. Sculpture and art also use symbols to tell stories. For example, among the Yorubas the leopard was king of all the creatures, so when the leopard appears in art or in storytelling, it symbolizes power.

As Nigerians struggled to break away from colonial rule, literature became a powerful tool, and writers used their talents to become a voice for independence. Later, after Nigeria became independent, some of the same writers used their words to criticize corruption and dictators who ruled by force.

Eyes on the Prize

Nigerian poet and playwright Wole Soyinka was born in 1934 to a Yoruba family. After attending school in Nigeria, where he was already winning prizes for his writing, he continued his studies in England and worked in the Royal Court Theatre in London. The plays he wrote were performed in both England and Nigeria. In many of his works, such as *The Strong Breed*, *The Road*, and *Death and the King's Horsemen*, he criticizes Nigerian society.

At the same time he was also active in Nigeria's struggle for independence from Great Britain. After Nigeria became independent, Soyinka was a continual voice criticizing the country's military dictators. During the Nigerian Civil War in 1967, he was arrested and imprisoned for two years for his political activities and his writings, many of which were critical of the government's oppression and corruption. When civilian rule was restored, he returned to Nigeria, but was forced to leave again in 1993, early in the regime of General Sani Abacha, when he escaped from Nigeria on a motorcycle and came to the United States. He has taught at many different universities in the United States, including Harvard and Yale. In 1994 he was appointed

UNESCO (United Nations Educational, Scientific and Cultural Organization) Goodwill Ambassador for the promotion of African culture, human rights, and freedom of expression. In 1986, he received the world's highest literary honor, the Nobel Prize in Literature. He was the first African ever to receive the award.

Perhaps the most important of these crusading writers was Wole Soyinka, who was jailed and exiled for his work.

Other Nigerian writers have gained worldwide attention and readers, including Ben Okri, who won the Man Booker Prize in 1991 for his book *The Famished Road*. Chinua Achebe's book *Things Fall Apart* has sold millions of copies, and uses traditional local life as its theme.

CHAPTER 10

Living in Nigeria

IN NIGERIA, HOMES IN CITIES ARE VERY DIFFERENT FROM those in rural areas. Wealthier neighborhoods in and around cities have apartment buildings and individual homes that look very much like ones found in North America. Some cities have public housing complexes. A large number of people live in shantytowns just outside the city, which are neighborhoods of shacks made from whatever materials could be scavenged.

Rural homes are different from one area to the next. Most regions use a basic structure made of mud bricks, and some buildings are reinforced with an outer wall of concrete. In the dry north, roofs may be flat and made out of mud, too, but in most other places roofs are made of grass thatch or woven mats. They are sloped to allow water to run off. In the south along the coast, many people build their homes out of raffia.

Opposite: **A couple in front of their home in southern Nigeria.**

With the electricity out, lanterns provide the light in a market where a woman is selling cassava flour.

Power and the People

Nigeria's power grid, the system that delivers electricity to its users, has not been maintained or expanded to meet the needs of a rapidly growing population. Even though Nigeria has an enormous amount of fuel available, its power plants do not produce enough electricity for everyone. It is common for the power to go out for hours or even sometimes days without any notice, even in government buildings and large urban centers. Rural areas do not have electricity at all unless it is produced by a generator, and this is rare.

Because of this, Nigerians do not depend heavily on things that require electricity. There are plenty of homes with televisions, and many more with radios, but these are not as central to life in Nigeria as they are in many other parts of the world. Lack of electricity is much more than an inconvenience. Not having dependable refrigeration to keep food from spoiling is a constant problem, and hospitals cannot depend on generators for extended periods.

The Quest for Water

Most Nigerians do not have running water in their homes, and have to transport it for their daily needs. Getting water can be as simple as bringing a bucket to a well or spigot, or as difficult as walking miles to the closest stream and back. More than fifty-six million Nigerians do not have access to an improved drinking water source. Lack of clean, safe water

A man sells water on the streets of Maiduguri, a city in northeastern Nigeria.

Children fill buckets from a rainwater tank in Nigeria.

is one of the biggest health threats in Nigeria and is a daily challenge.

Water that stands for any period of time, especially in hot climates, can quickly become a breeding ground for bacteria and disease. Water taken from streams and rivers is usually polluted by the people upstream, because it is also being used for washing, bathing, and waste disposal. Even public water systems and wells are often polluted by human and animal waste that seeps into the ground. Most rural homes, and even many in urban areas, have water-collecting containers called cisterns, which provide rainwater that can be used for drinking after it is boiled or filtered. This is one of the cleanest sources of water available to Nigerians.

National Holidays

New Year's Day	January 1
Good Friday	March or April
Easter Monday	March or April
Workers' Day	May 1
Democracy Day	May 29
Independence Day	October 1
Christmas Day	December 25
Boxing Day	December 26

Several Muslim holidays are also national holidays. Because the Islamic calendar is eleven days shorter than the Western calendar, the date of these holidays moves each year:

Mawlid

Eid al-Fitr

Eid al-Adha

Favorite Foods

Like everything else in Nigeria, the foods people eat every day vary by region and ethnic group. But they share many common ingredients that are grown in farms and gardens or are easy to buy in the markets, such as rice, peanuts, yams, corn, beans, pumpkin, tomatoes, and a starchy root called cassava.

Northern Nigerians raise a lot of beef, and people all over Nigeria raise chickens and goats, so these are popular meats. Because Nigeria is a tropical country, it has a lot of fruit, such as pineapples, oranges, mangoes, papayas, and bananas. Many dishes are seasoned with hot chili peppers, sometimes quite a lot of them!

Popular rice dishes are coconut rice, fried rice, and Jollof rice, a dish made with tomatoes, spices, and seafood that is

Jollof rice is often served with chicken.

often served at parties and weddings. Meats are often grilled, sometimes on a stick. One of the most popular meals all over Nigeria is *suya*, grilled meat that is coated with powdered chili and other spices. *Kilishi* is thinly sliced meat that has been dried and coated with a chili paste before being grilled briefly. In southeastern Nigeria, common dishes include *nkwobi*, beef cooked in a rich spicy sauce, and *afang*, a vegetable soup. Among the Yorubas, *efo riro* is a favorite soup made with leafy greens that is eaten with fish.

Markets and Food Carts

Most people in villages and small towns, and even many people in cities, shop in open markets where they buy directly from farmers and small vendors. In these markets, as well as

Coconut Rice

Coconut rice is a popular dish, and there are many recipes for it. Some add chopped vegetables or hot peppers. This is a simple version, and it's simply delicious. Have an adult help you.

Ingredients

1 cup white rice

2 cups cold water

¼ cup vegetable oil

1 small onion, chopped small

1 large can diced tomatoes

1 can coconut milk (15 ounces)

1 teaspoon salt

Directions

Boil the rice in water for about 10 to 12 minutes (it should not be completely soft). Meanwhile, heat the vegetable oil in a saucepan. Add the onions and stir for a minute or two over low heat. Add the tomatoes, coconut milk, and salt. Cover and cook for about 5 to 7 minutes, until the mixture boils. Then add the rice. Stir the mixture, cover it, and then let it simmer until the rice is almost dry and has absorbed all the juices. Enjoy!

Men in Katsina roast meat to make suya, a popular street food.

along the streets, people sell snacks and foods cooked over makeshift stoves and grills. With more than half of Nigerians living in poverty, these pop-up stands are a source of inexpensive, nourishing food.

Grilled fish, suya, *moyi-moyi* (a bean cake wrapped in leaves that is a Yoruba specialty), deep-fried yams, little meat pies, and stews are common favorites. Plantain chips and fried sweet dough, called puff-puff, are common street snacks.

Going to School

By law, every child in Nigeria must attend school for at least nine years: six years in primary school and three in junior secondary school. Some Nigerians are able to continue their education and go on to senior secondary school, which lasts an additional three years. Beyond that, students may continue on to college for a four-year degree or go to a technical school.

The federal and local governments provide primary and secondary schools, and the federal government runs most of the large universities and technical schools.

The average child does not spend more than the nine required years in school. Unfortunately, many do not even spend nine years in school because they are forced to work instead. In northeastern Nigeria, most schools have closed entirely because of the constant threats from Boko Haram. In these cases, families do the best they can to educate their children at home. Today, about 50 percent of Nigerian women and 70 of Nigerian men can read and write.

Girls at a private school in southwestern Nigeria. Some Nigerians believe the quality of public schools has declined significantly in recent years, so they pay to send their children to private school.

Nigerian boys play soccer on the beach.

Sports for Life

Soccer, which Nigerians call football, is a national passion. Children barely old enough to run are already kicking soccer balls in the streets of every town. School soccer teams are very competitive and are the training ground for Nigeria's professional teams.

The Nigerian national football team is called the Super Eagles, and has been the African champion three times. In 1994, the Super Eagles were ranked fifth in the world, the highest place ever reached by an African soccer team.

In 1996, Nigeria surprised the whole world by winning the gold medal for soccer at the Summer Olympics. The Nigerian team was not expected to beat such powerful teams as Brazil and Argentina. This was one of two gold medals Nigeria took home in the 1996 Olympics. Chioma Ajunwa also won the gold medal in the long jump. The women's national soccer team, the Super Falcons, has set records, too, winning the first seven African championships.

Nigerians in the NBA

Numerous Nigerians have played in the NBA, the professional basketball league in the United States. They include:

Hakeem Olajuwon: (right, number 34) 7 foot 0 inches (2.13 m) tall; Houston Rockets (1984–2001), Toronto Raptors (2001–2002)

Yinka Dare: 7 foot 0 inches (2.13 m) tall; New Jersey Nets (1994–1998)

Olumide Oyedeji: 6 foot 10.75 inches (2.10 m) tall; Seattle SuperSonics (2000–2002), Orlando Magic (2002–2003)

Solomon Alabi: 7 foot 1 inch (2.16 m) tall; Toronto Raptors (2010–2012)

Festus Ezeli: 6 foot 11 inches (2.11 m) tall; Golden State Warriors (2012–)

A third team, the Golden Eaglets, is Nigeria's national soccer team for players under seventeen years old. This team has won the world title five times, most recently in 2015. Nigeria is the first country to win the title five times.

Basketball is also a popular sport in Nigeria and the national team, nicknamed D'Tigers, is one of the best national basketball teams in Africa. In 2015 Nigeria's team won the African basketball championships. Both the men's and women's basketball teams have competed in the Summer Olympics, but have never won a medal.

Regardless of whether they win or lose, Nigerians follow the games intently and cheer on their teams enthusiastically, proud of what they have achieved and looking forward to better days ahead.

Timeline

NIGERIAN HISTORY			WORLD HISTORY
Early humans inhabit what is now Nigeria.	9000 BCE		
		ca. 2500 BCE	The Egyptians build the pyramids and the Sphinx in Giza.
The Nok people settle on the Jos Plateau.	500 BCE	ca. 563 BCE	The Buddha is born in India.
		313 CE	The Roman emperor Constantine legalizes Christianity.
The Igbo-Ukwu settle the northern Niger Delta.	900 CE	610	The Prophet Muhammad begins preaching a new religion called Islam.
		1054	The Eastern (Orthodox) and Western (Roman Catholic) Churches break apart.
		1095	The Crusades begin.
		1215	King John seals the Magna Carta.
The Oyo settle the western region; the Benin Kingdom rises to power.	1300s	1300s	The Renaissance begins in Italy.
		1347	The plague sweeps through Europe.
		1453	Ottoman Turks capture Constantinople, conquering the Byzantine Empire.
Portuguese traders encounter the Benin people; the European slave trade begins.	1470s	1492	Columbus arrives in North America.
		1500s	Reformers break away from the Catholic Church, and Protestantism is born.
Olaudah Equiano purchases his freedom and publishes his influential work on abolition.	1766	1776	The U.S. Declaration of Independence is signed.
Usman dan Fodio launches a jihad that unites the north as an Islamic state.	1804	1789	The French Revolution begins.
Britain abolishes the slave trade.	1807		
The Royal Niger Company is formed to oversee trade in the Niger Delta.	1886	1865	The American Civil War ends.
Most of modern-day Nigeria is under British control.	1905	1879	The first practical lightbulb is invented.

NIGERIAN HISTORY

Britain declares the region the Colony and Protectorate of Nigeria.	**1914**
Herbert Macaulay establishes the Nigerian National Democratic Party, starting the Pan-Africanism movement.	**1923**
Macaulay unites dozens of groups into the National Council of Nigeria and the Cameroons.	**1944**
Oil is discovered in the Niger Delta.	**1956**
Nigeria becomes independent.	**1960**
The country is declared the Federal Republic of Nigeria.	**1963**
A military coup topples Prime Minister Abubakar Balewa.	**1966**
The Eastern Region separates from Nigeria, calling itself the Republic of Biafra; a civil war follows.	**1967**
Biafra loses the civil war and reunifies with Nigeria.	**1970**
General Murtala Ramat Mohammed overthrows a military regime.	**1975**
Major General Muhammadu Buhari leads a military coup and takes control of Nigeria.	**1983**
Presidential elections are voided, the government is overthrown, General Sani Abacha takes control.	**1993**
Olusegun Obasanjo wins a peaceful election and takes over as civilian president.	**1999**
President Goodluck Jonathan declares a state of emergency as a result of Boko Haram attacks.	**2013**
Boko Haram kidnaps 276 girls from a school.	**2014**

WORLD HISTORY

1914	World War I begins.
1917	The Bolshevik Revolution brings communism to Russia.
1929	A worldwide economic depression begins.
1939	World War II begins.
1945	World War II ends.
1969	Humans land on the Moon.
1975	The Vietnam War ends.
1989	The Berlin Wall is torn down as communism crumbles in Eastern Europe.
1991	The Soviet Union breaks into separate states.
2001	Terrorists attack the World Trade Center in New York City and the Pentagon near Washington, D.C.
2004	A tsunami in the Indian Ocean destroys coastlines in Africa, India, and Southeast Asia.
2008	The United States elects its first African American president.

Fast Facts

Official name: Federal Republic of Nigeria

Capital: Abuja

Official language: English

Official religion: None

Year of independence: 1960

Lagos

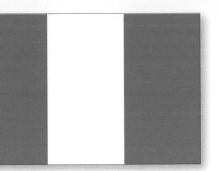

National flag

National anthem:	"Arise, O Compatriots"
Type of government:	Federal republic
Head of state:	President
Head of government:	President
Area:	356,669 square miles (923,768 sq km)
Latitude and longitude of geographic center:	10° 00' N, 8° 00' E
Bordering countries:	Benin Republic to the west, the Republic of Niger to the north, Cameroon to the east, and Chad to the northeast
Highest elevation:	Chappal Waddi, 7,936 feet (2,419 m) above sea level
Lowest elevation:	Sea level along the coast
Average high temperature:	In Lagos, 90°F (32°C) in January; 82°F (28°C) in July
Average low temperature:	In Lagos, 72°F (22°C) in January; 72°F (22°C) in July
Average annual precipitation:	Varies, from 20 inches (50 cm) in the far north to 120 inches (300 cm) in the southeast

Niger River

Emir's Palace

Currency

National population (2015 est.): 181,562,056

Population of largest cities (2015 est.):

Lagos	13,123,000
Kano	3,587,000
Ibadan	3,160,000
Abuja	2,440,000
Port Harcourt	2,343,000

Landmarks:
▶ *Cross River National Park*, in Cross River State

▶ *Emir's Palace*, Kano

▶ *Nigerian National Museum*, Lagos

▶ *Yankari National Park*, Bauchi State

▶ *Zuma Rock*, Abuja

Economy: Nigeria's biggest industry is oil, which accounts for about 95 percent of Nigeria's income from exports. Nigeria is the fifth-largest oil exporting country in the world. Nigeria also has vast natural gas reserves and exports agricultural products such as rubber and cocoa beans.

Currency: Naira. In 2016, 199 naira equaled US$1.00.

System of weights and measures: Metric system

Literacy rate (2015): 59.6%

Schoolchildren

Nigerian words and phrases:

English	Yoruba	Igbo	Hausa
Good morning	Ekuojumo	Igbolachi	Ina kwana
Good night	Odaaro	Kachifo	Said a safe
How are you?	Se daadaa ni?	Kedu ka idi?	Kana Lafiya?
Thank you	E se	Dalu	Nagode

Prominent Nigerians:

Chinua Achebe (1930–2013)
Novelist

King Sunny Ade (1946–)
Musician

Chioma Ajunwa (1970–)
Olympic athlete

Queen Amina (1563–1610)
Hausa leader

Olaudah Equiano (1745–1797)
Abolitionist

Fela Kuti (1938–1997)
Musician

Ben Okri (1959–)
Poet and novelist

Wole Soyinka (1934–)
Nobel Prize–winning playwright

Wole Soyinka

To Find Out More

Books

▶ Hahner-Herzog, Iris, Maria Kecskesi, and Laszlo Vajda. *African Masks: From the Barbier-Mueller Collection*. New York: Prestel Publishing, 2010.

▶ Lemieux, Diane. *Nigeria*. London: Kuperard, 2012.

▶ McKenna, Amy (ed). *The History of Western Africa*. New York: Rosen Publishing, 2011.

Music

▶ Adé, King Sunny. *Juju Music*. San Francisco: INgrooves Music Group, 1990.

▶ Kuti, Fela. *The Best of the Black President*. Brooklyn, NY: Knitting Factory Records, 2009.

▶ *The Rough Guide to the Music of Nigeria & Ghana*. London: World Music Network, 2002.

▶ Visit this Scholastic Web site for more information on Nigeria:
www.factsfornow.scholastic.com
Enter the keyword Nigeria

Index

Page numbers in *italics* indicate illustrations.

Burutu, 74

Z

Meet the Author

Lura Rogers Seavey studied at Skidmore College in New York and Harvard University in Massachusetts, where she received a Bachelor of Arts degree. She has written several other books in the Enchantment of the World series, including *Spain*, *Switzerland*, and *Dominican Republic*. She is also the author of *More Than Petticoats: Remarkable Massachusetts Women*, a collection of short biographies.

Photo Credits